Praise for

Coming Clean

"Reality shows typically stay with hoarders only long enough to portray them as objects of pity or ridicule, but Miller's story, *Coming Clean*, offers a uniquely nuanced look at her intelligent, loving, but broken father and the enduring effect his affliction has had on her and her long-suffering mother." — *Entertainment Weekly*

"[Kimberly Rae Miller] recounts a childhood in which it was impossible to shower in her house or cook in the kitchen, of being bitten by fleas and listening to rats rustle at night. The hoarding surrounds everything . . . This searing tale of the damage caused by the disease reflects Miller's deep consideration of her experience; it is a deeply affecting, remarkably thoughtful, and well-reasoned book, yet the horror is always there. One can only admire Miller's courage in coming clean." — *Booklist*, starred review

"Stuff and unused purchases were piled so high that little room was left for the family even to eat or sleep or use the bathrooms . . . As a child Miller realized her family wasn't like other people's families with tidy, presentable homes; far from it . . . Miller never invited anyone home and had to adopt a 'decoy' house to be dropped off at by friends." — *Publishers Weekly*

"[An] honest, sensitive memoir . . . At the heart of *Coming Clean* . . . lie two equally mysterious phenomena, one as timely as the other is timeless. Hoarding, the first, has only recently entered the popular lexicon while the second, familial love, spans the ages."
— *Washington Independent Review of Books*

"Miller renders her harrowing account without self-pity, and her empathy for her parents, as well as her refusal to treat the hoarding as a spectacle, allow space for redemption — both theirs and her own." — *Elle*

"Kimberly Rae Miller writes with insight about growing up the daughter of a hoarder in her family's moldy, flea-infested home — and eventually overcoming her anger and shame." — *Parade*

"An engrossing, sympathetic exploration of living with hoarder parents." — *Kirkus Reviews*

"Kimberly Rae Miller's new memoir comes clean on how the reality of compulsive hoarding is very different from what we see on TV . . . Astonishingly honest and heartfelt." — *Daily Beast*

"*Coming Clean* is shocking and painful . . . But it's also full of warmth and compassion, in some ways a tribute to Miller's deeply imperfect parents." — *PureWow*

"Miller's wry retelling of her upbringing . . . will encourage others who also did not emerge from the cookie cutter." — *Library Journal*

"Turn off the reality TV and read *Coming Clean*, an engrossing, beautifully written memoir of growing up in a hoarding family that treats its subject with humanity and grace."
— Doreen Orion, author of *Queen of the Road*

Coming Clean

Coming Clean

Kimberly Rae Miller

New Harvest
Houghton Mifflin Harcourt
BOSTON   NEW YORK

First paperback edition 2014
Copyright © 2013 by Kimberly Rae Miller

This edition published by special arrangement with Amazon Publishing

For information about permission to reproduce
selections from this book, go to www.apub.com.

www.hmhco.com

Library of Congress Cataloging-in-Publication Data
Miller, Kimberly Rae.
Coming clean / Kimberly Rae Miller.
pages cm
ISBN 978-0-544-02583-7 (hardback) ISBN 978-0-544-32081-9 (pbk.)
1. Miller, Kimberly Rae — Childhood and youth. 2. Authors — United States — Biography.
3. Compulsive hoarding. I. Title.
CT275.M5148A3 2013
973.92′092 — dc23
[B]   2013010483

Book design by Brian Moore

Printed in the United States of America
DOC 10 9 8 7 6 5 4 3 2 1

Names and minor identifying details of friends, family, and
medical professionals have been changed to protect their privacy.

To Mom and Dad, I love you bigger than the world.

Kim, Age 9, Long Island
Courtesy of the Miller family

What shames us, what we most fear to tell, does not set us apart from others; it binds us together if only we can take the risk to speak it.

— STARHAWK

Coming Clean

The Art of the *a*

I HAVE A BOX where I keep all of the holiday and birthday and just-because cards that my friends and family send me. They are memories, tokens of love and thoughtfulness, and there is a part of me that can't bear to throw them out.

I don't need these cards. I hardly ever open that box, and so they don't add anything to my life, but there is a part of me that thinks that maybe, just maybe, one day I will need to remember the moments and people they represent.

This is as close as I can come to understanding the way my father thinks. He loves paper and pens and radios and things that are broken and things that are cheap and things that remind him of things that he once liked and things that remind him of me and of things that I once liked — in that same can't-bear-to-let-it-go way I feel about those cards. He sees a thousand tangential futures for a broken radio, articles he has yet to read in a nine-year-old issue of the *New York Times,* and one specific memory for that glittery purple pencil he writes notes in his planner with. He used a similarly purple pencil that one time I came home crying from school because I couldn't write a lowercase *A.* I sat on his lap and we spent what felt like hours writing little Os with tails until I finally mastered the art of the a.

My father is a hoarder. I can say that now, and people's eyes widen in understanding. Maybe they know someone who is a hoarder, or maybe they throw that word around to describe their messy roommate, but hoarder is now a part of our common vernacular.

As ubiquitous as it may seem, it's still a relatively new word. When I was growing up, there was no defining term for why my father loved stuff so much. I certainly couldn't imagine anyone else in the world living the way my family did. None of my friends abandoned entire rooms of their house to the things that lived there. They weren't pushed off couches or beds by piles of clothes and papers and knickknacks, with the resolution to find somewhere else to sit or sleep in the future.

I stopped thinking about the house I grew up in almost as soon as I left it at eighteen. I didn't forget or block it out; I just simply decided not to remember. By that time my parents were in a new home — a messy, more than messy, but not as messy home. And then eight years of not-remembering later, in the middle of my clean little grown-up life, I started having nightmares.

In these dreams I am always gearing up to clean. I don't know where to start and so I do what I always do when I want to avoid work: I go get a snack. In one particular dream I am trudging barefoot through the downstairs hallway, then the den, and eventually the kitchen. I can feel the wet mashed newspapers between my toes, not so different from the way sand feels as you inch closer to the ocean. I tiptoe around the debris in my path, conscious that there is probably something sharp amidst the sludge, paper, and old clothing. As I rummage through the kitchen I am keenly aware that I do not want to open the refrigerator. It has been abandoned for years, and what exists inside is a soupy mess of rotting food. Instead, I scour the counter for packaged foods. In the bread box there is what was once a loaf of Wonder Bread, but is now a shrunken heap of moss and maggots. Ramen soup is safe, I think, but when I open the package there are bugs inside that, too.

The bugs don't faze me in my dream, as they didn't faze me in my adolescence, and I put the bug-infested bag of soup mix back on the counter. I don't throw it out because there's really no point anymore.

It's not always the kitchen. Sometimes I'm in the bathroom, or the hallway, or the living room. Each room has its own particular flavor of squalor, but what remains constant is that I am always trying to figure out where and how to start to fix it.

These are the kind of dreams that jar me from my sleep in the middle of the night. My mind doesn't always catch up with my body, and it takes me a minute or so to realize that I'm not at the house in the middle-class suburbs of Long Island that I grew up in but the small, neat Brooklyn apartment I have called home for the whole of my adult life. My first instinct, once my bearings have been located, is to call my mom. She is quite possibly the only person who understands how deeply these scars run, and I need her to tell me that this is not my life anymore, and that it never will be again. I know she will, and then she will apologize, as she always does. She has been apologizing for as long as I can remember, but I can never forgive her enough for her to forgive herself. She has always been afraid of dreams like these, afraid that a last straw would come along and I would stop loving her.

She has warned me, "One day you won't be able to pretend everything was okay, and you're going to hate us."

My mother is right more often than not, and she is right that everything was not okay. The memories are still there in the place in my mind I put them years ago, but the person in them doesn't feel like me at all. She feels like a younger sister, someone close to me, someone I want to reach out to, to tell her that her world will be better. And cleaner. I've been there, I've seen it, and it turns out normally ever after for her.

But my mother is wrong about one thing: I do not hate her or my father. Sure, I remember the dirt and the rats and the squalor, but I also remember parents who loved me. Doting, fallible people who gave me everything they had, and a whole lot more.

South Shore

ONE

H E HAD ONE PLASTIC BAG tied to another tied to a
torn knapsack and rested it all on his shoulders. This
man was mesmerizing. This man was homeless. I had
never thought about homeless people before, but I knew that
was what he was.

I craned my neck backward to watch him, my mother pulling
me toward our gate, as he walked through Penn Station and ate
the remnants of a box of Kentucky Fried Chicken. I wondered
how he had paid for his chicken and watched as his plastic bags
swayed from side to side with each of his steps.

When he saw me staring he tilted his box of chicken toward
me in offering, and I immediately looked away and ran to catch
up with my mother. I didn't look back, but I thought about him
the whole ride home.

"Are you feeling okay?" My mom asked as she bent over to
kiss my forehead. "You don't have a fever."

I wasn't usually quiet, at least not around my parents, and
whenever I was speechless for more than a few minutes at a time
my parents assumed that I wasn't feeling well. I nodded my head
to indicate that I was fine. I wasn't, but the bad feeling wasn't

sickness — it was something else. The man in the train station, with his tattered appearance, bags of trash, and kind offering, reminded me of my father.

My dad wasn't like other people. He didn't follow the rules that seemed to govern other grown-ups, and the priorities that he tethered himself to were ideas and knowledge, mostly in the form of newspapers and books, reinforced by a steady soundtrack of NPR. He did the things that other adults did: He had a family, he had a job, but even when I was a little girl they seemed to me like accidental realities he had stumbled into.

I never doubted his love for me but was always slightly afraid that he would get distracted one day and forget about our life. He might trail off in the direction of a shiny new thought and end up like the man in Penn Station, content to wander the corridors of the world with bags of papers to keep him company.

At the end of the two-hour train ride home to Long Island, I saw my dad out the window, waiting at the curb of the station for us in our baby blue Mercury Zephyr. Dutifully, he left the driver's seat to open up the back door for me. I ran up to him, and in his usual greeting he threw me over his shoulder, fireman-style. He turned around quickly, asking "K-Rae, where'd you go? You were right here."

"I'm behind you," was my answer — it always was — and when he turned around again I was still behind him, my hands anchored into the back pockets of his jeans to ground myself. This went on for three or four turns, both of us laughing, before my mother reminded us that we were in a parking lot and I officially ended our game.

"I am over your shoulder! Please put me down." These two

sentences had been established through routine as the game-ender.

A feigned double-take and an "Oh, there you are" later, he was buckling me in the seat behind my mother. He had to push aside the shiny loose pages torn from waiting-room magazines, old newspapers, empty cups, and long-ago-used bottles of motor oil and funnels that lived in the backseat to make room for me. He sang the seatbelt song as he buckled me in, as was my rule. If this particular ritual was not done to my liking, I would unbuckle my seatbelt as soon as the car was in motion.

> *Buckle up for safety, buckle up!*
> *Buckle up for safety, always buckle up!*

"I can't believe you're making your daughter sit in garbage," my mother said.

> *Show the world you care by the belt you wear.*
> *Buckle up for safety, everybody, buckle up!*

"You had all day to clean the car out, Brian!"
My father said nothing as he returned to the driver's seat. Instead, he turned on the car radio and let the news answer for him.

TWO

WHEN I WAS BORN, my grandparents ordered little bottles of champagne with my name, weight, and birth date on them.

Brian & Nora proudly announce the birth of their daughter:
Kimberly Rae Miller
December 23, 1982
10:49am   3lb. 2 oz.

They waited until I was two months old to hand them out to family and friends; they waited until they were sure I would live. I was born three months early, just like my father had been. The doctors told my parents that premature birth doesn't run in families, but my father and I have always had a striking number of similarities: same IQ, 138; same Chinese horoscope, Year of the Dog; same inability to understand why anyone would eat caramel of their own volition.

My mother kept the makeup mirror in the passenger seat's visor angled so she could watch me in the backseat while my father drove us around. She didn't drive; she had a license and technically knew how, but was always phobic behind the wheel. Her fear hadn't much affected her life until she and my father decided to leave the Bronx, their mutual hometown, in favor of suburban living a few years before I was born. She often said she felt like a prisoner on Long Island, dependent on my father to take her everywhere, but New York City during the 1980s wasn't a safe place to raise a family anymore — at least not the part where we could afford to live.

I could see that she was watching me — her eyes reflecting back to me in the mirror. With a captive audience, I asked for her to tell me the story of my birth. It was a story I wanted to hear as often as possible. Without fail, she would start each recitation by telling me I was her miracle baby. I took the definition seriously, as if it were a job title, and always studied her story for clues about my miraculous nature.

Two days before Christmas, her water broke while she was in the shower. She didn't realize what had happened, so she called her own mother to ask what labor felt like. "I don't remember, it was a long time ago," was my grandmother's response. My mother had never been pregnant before, and I wasn't due until March, so she assumed that this was just a normal part of pregnancy and went about getting ready for work. At the time my parents worked at the same civil service job and drove into Manhattan together each morning.

"We were halfway to the city when I realized your foot was starting to crown," she told me. "I called my doctor, who was on vacation playing golf somewhere, and he told me to turn around and go to Stony Brook University Hospital, because they had a NICU."

This is where my father would chime in with his own details about the indignity of not being allowed in the delivery room. The size and shape of the window through which he watched the action unravel changed by the telling; sometimes it was a circle, sometimes a diamond, sometimes there was no window at all and he had to peek through the crack in the door.

"I heard your mother yelling at the doctors," he laughed.

"They called you an '*it*,'" my mother said. "They said 'It's out!' and I sat up and said 'She is not an *it*, her name is Kimberly Rae.'" Up until that moment I was either going to be Jennifer Simone or Kimberly Rae. My fate was decided by a split-second decision dictated solely by anger.

"I only wanted a girl. If you were a boy, I would have sold you," she told me, and I believed her. I would have been named Eric if I was a boy. A boy named Eric who was sold for not being a girl. I looked like my father, with blond hair, blue eyes, and a round face; I imagined that Eric looked like my mom — short, with brown eyes and kinky red hair.

At the end of it all, my father said they rushed me out of the delivery room and he ran after them yelling, "Wait, that's mine!"

That was my favorite part.

It took my parents two years to get pregnant. Her doctor had prescribed fertility drugs, but my mother refused to take them, afraid that she would have twins or triplets. "I wasn't sure I could love more than one child," she said. "My mother couldn't."

My mother and grandmother weren't particularly fond of each other, and from what I could tell their tenuous relationship started to deteriorate when my mother was five years old and her sister, Lee, was born. She never resented Lee for it, but she resented her parents.

My grandparents came to the hospital a week after I was born, and according to my mother my grandmother's only words of motherly advice were, "She's probably going to die. Best not to get too attached." This particular part of the story was never spared, and no matter how many times my mother told me the story of my birth, she never stopped being mad when she got to that part.

"We weren't sure that you were going to live, but while you were here we wanted you to know that you were loved."

The rest of the story was recited like a checklist of trials they were asked to endure. They weren't allowed to hold me or feed me, but she and my father sat by my incubator talking to me. I would "forget to breathe" she said, and a nurse would have to come along and remind me by shaking my arm or leg. If I went ten days without forgetting, I could go home, but I had an uncanny habit of forgetting every ninth day.

There was the one time that she and my father came to visit after work and saw me with a needle sticking out of my head. My mother turned and walked away, not wanting me to see her cry. Eventually she would force herself to come back; there were other babies, she said, whose parents didn't come every day. And those were the babies who died. "They needed someone to live for," she told me. "And no one was there." She and my father never missed visiting hours.

I believed with every telling of this story that my parents loved me into living, that the three of us were meant to be a family, and that I was going to be a miracle, if I could only figure out how.

THREE

"MRS. AND MR. MILLER, thank you for coming in," Ms. Angela, my nursery school teacher said. She shifted in her seat, leaning forward to deliver the bad news in a nose-scrunching whisper. "Kimberly has been excusing herself to go to the bathroom to masturbate."

Earlier that week, Ms. A had come into the bathroom only to find me shoving a blue plastic soda bottle into my underpants.

My father choked on his tea, holding back a laugh, and then raised an eyebrow in my direction; my mother didn't flinch. She knew exactly what was happening. "She's not masturbating. She's robbing you."

I feigned distraction. While the grown-ups talked, I placed myself at the toy station most convenient for eavesdropping, occupying my hands with Weeble Wobbles, but soaking in everything being said about me. I needed to gauge what kind of trouble I was going to be in. I wasn't particularly concerned with my parents; at most, we'd sit down when we got home and have a tedious conversation about why my little problem was unhygienic, immoral, and unfair to the other preschoolers in my class. Ms. Angela and the rest of the nursery school staff were my concern; I wanted them to like me.

My logic was simple. If I put something that I wanted in my underpants, even if I was caught, I'd be allowed to keep it. It had my vagina germs on it.

"Kimberly, were you putting toys in your underpants?" Ms. Angela asked me sweetly.

"No?" Acting innocent and confused was my general strategy for adult confrontations. That, or blaming a dog. This time, there were no dogs around. It was my word against my mother's.

She turned back to my parents and, as if she were informing them that the sky was blue, said, "Mr. and Mrs. Miller, children don't lie."

I liked that Ms. A had my back, but knew my parents weren't buying it. My attention shifted to the parking lot. Outside the big glass doors was a Jeep, the kind that on top is a normal-sized truck, but on bottom has giant wheels. I wanted that truck. If that were our truck, all the other kids would be jealous. People would stare at us, they'd want to be us, and then we could run over their cars.

"We have a Monster Truck," I announced to no one in particular. I wanted to try on what it felt like to say that.

As the opportunity to prove her point arose, my mother schooled my teacher. "We drive a Mercury, Ms. Angela. A Mercury on Mercury-sized tires. She's lying, because that's what children do."

We left before Ms. Angela could come up with some sort of retort. In the parking lot, my mother informed me that I would have to give back everything I'd taken, and "Stop putting things in your underpants!"

My dad just grinned, and sipped his tea.

I was allowed back to nursery school the following week, but my credibility and access to the toy box were shot. Luckily, kindergarten was starting in a month, and I'd have new toys to pilfer.

My parents both took the day off from work to see me off on my first day of real school, armed with cameras and tissues and supportive smiles. While other kids cried outside our classroom, holding onto their mothers, I refused my parents entry into the school and assured them I'd see them afterward. New school. New toy box. I was ready. But once I was inside Mrs. White's kindergarten classroom, the anxiety started to settle in.

I didn't know anyone. I didn't know *how* to know anyone. In nursery school, I'd had Jacob. His parents were friends with mine, so we were friends by default. Since he was the only boy I knew, I planned on marrying him.

Jacob agreed, but only if he could also marry his friend Joanna. Because she had sisters, she'd inherited the motherload of Barbie clothes. Since I figured this arrangement could only serve to benefit my Barbies, I agreed to a life of polygamy.

There was no Jacob in kindergarten. Without a preexisting friend in place, I realized that I had nothing to say to the other kids. I liked grown-ups. Grown-ups and I had an understanding; they lavished me with attention, and I accepted it. Kids, on the other hand, just thought I was weird.

My parents didn't believe in baby talk. Instead they spoke to me like they would a well-educated yet slightly confused forty-year-old. While my vocabulary never ceased to impress their peers, my own looked at me as if I were speaking Farsi. I would often announce to the class that I had an "urgent need to urinate," or complain that I'd "suffered an abrasion" on the playground. I tried to blend in, but I could never bring myself to say "pee-pee" and "boo-boo" like my classmates did. It felt degrading. So I was mostly left to my own devices unless a game of house was short a person to act as the husband when all the more covetable roles in the family hierarchy had been doled out.

The first month of kindergarten was not everything I had dreamed it would be; for the most part, I was bored with the monotony of arts and crafts projects and rote recitations of numbers and letters. That is, until the day a month or so into the school year, when it was announced that each student would be meeting with the school's social worker.

I couldn't think of a more perfect way to spend an afternoon. An opportunity to do what I did best: Impress a grown-up.

One by one, my classmates were called to the front of the classroom, where they were whisked away by a smiling woman with long curly brown hair and two layers of bangs: one that lay flat across her forehead and another that fanned out on top of her head. I had no idea who she was, or how she got her hair to do that, but I had no doubt that we would get along smashingly.

While we recited the alphabet and listened to stories about friendly dinosaurs, my attention wandered endlessly back to the door. I imagined that each successive child was being escorted to some sort of exclusive club. A club where adults and children socialized as equals. A club where one could drink as much soda and eat as much candy as they wanted. A club that as of yet I had not been invited to join.

"Kimberly Miller?" a voice finally called. I immediately jumped up, and then, not to seem too excited, walked leisurely to the front door.

"I'm Kimberly Miller." I said quietly, and looked back at my class to see if anyone was looking at me. They weren't.

In the hallway, the woman with the bangs told me that her name was Ms. Russo and that she worked for the school, and just wanted to ask me some questions, "If that's okay?"

Not what I had been planning, but still better than coloring by myself. I immediately started going through my repertoire of crowd-pleasers in preparation to wow her and make her my friend; my dad had just taught me to spell "antidisestablishmentarianism," which never failed to impress, so I could do that, and I was taking karate so I could perform my *kata* for her. And if there was room enough, I could show her what I was learning in dance school. She could then tell me how smart and pretty I was. This was going to be fun.

Ms. Russo and I walked through a part of the school I had never seen before. This was big-kid territory, and intimidating. The paintings that lined the walls here were neater; these were kids who had mastered the art of coloring within the confines of the lines or, even more awe-inspiring, without any lines at all. The unfamiliar setting and the fact that our conversation seemed to have hit a standstill started to make me antsy.

Our walk ended when we arrived at a small brick room with gray painted walls. Ms. Russo ushered me inside and sat across from me at the tyke-sized table, opened a manila folder, and as if on cue, smiled again.

With her knees bent high into her torso, Ms. Russo started

to ask me questions about life as a five-year-old. Did I know my address? Did I have a bedtime? Did I have any pets?

I answered, but with each question I elaborated a bit more, trying to get a conversation going: *Someone had been murdered on my block. I got to hold a newborn puppy once. In Alaska, night-time can last for twenty-four hours, and Eskimos eat a lot of fat to stay warm in the winter, but my mom cut the fat off of my meat because we aren't Eskimos.* But each time Ms. Russo would just smile and then curtly ask me another pointed question.

My efforts to impress her appeared to be failing miserably. And then the topic of siblings came up. "Yes, I have a sister. Her name is Sheryl."

The more questions she asked about Sheryl, the more I told her.

I wasn't sure how old Sheryl was. She was a baby, I guessed. She was often naked, I explained, because there was only one dress that fit her, and sometimes it had to be sacrificed to the greater good of my stuffed panda named Male Panda or one of my cocker spaniels.

Ms. Russo's initial indifference toward me was transforming into undivided attention.

"Tell me more about Sheryl."

"Dad puts her in the trunk when we go shopping," I vented. This had been a point of contention in our family for some time now, or at least the last few weeks. I wanted Sheryl to go with me everywhere, but my parents wanted to stop going on Sheryl scavenger hunts when I would inevitably lose her somewhere.

It was obvious by her disapproving looks and spirited scrib-bling that Ms. Russo agreed with me. My parents were being completely unreasonable.

The more intently my new friend listened to my stories, the more I continued to divulge my exasperation toward my parents' handling of my little sister.

"Faith urinated on her."

"Who is Faith, Kimberly?"

"Our dog." Ms. Russo was not keeping up with the conversation.

I told her about the long night Sheryl had spent soaking in a suds-bath in the bathroom sink and continued from there to air my most recent grievance: Sheryl had been taken away from me as punishment for stealing those toys from the nursery school.

My enthusiasm eventually waned. This wasn't quite as fun as I'd imagined, and I didn't want to be late for the milk lady, lest all the chocolate milk be taken. Ms. Russo walked me back to my classroom. She took my kindergarten teacher aside while I joined the rest of the class in playtime. I was sure she was explaining how gifted I was.

That day, when my babysitter came to pick me up from school, her infant daughter Kaitlynn on her hip, my teacher came running out and demanded to know if the little girl was Sheryl.

Within days of my meeting with Ms. Russo, the mood at home changed. My parents started fighting more, taking days at a time off from work, and cleaning well past the time that I went to bed. My father was messy. So messy I didn't know the color of our carpets. Paper covered the dining room table, the couch, the bathroom floor. Old newspapers lined the floor of my bedroom. And now, according to my mother, someone was coming to the house to check on me and Sheryl, someone who would see how messy he was.

Our home was of the ticky-tacky Levitt variety. Every house

on our block looked the same — except we never opened our shades, our plants were a little more unkempt, and the neighbors never came over for a cup of coffee.

Our house was two stories tall, but the second floor was like a forbidden wonderland to me. We didn't use it. In fact, I often forgot it was there. One room was dubbed the Bird Room because it was filled with birds: cockatiels, parakeets, and English budgies, all housed with another of their kind in arranged marriages, with the hope that nature would prevail and tiny featherless offspring would be produced. My parents would then sell the baby birds at local pet stores and flea markets. The brown carpets of the Bird Room were covered in bird seed, discarded feathers, and puffs of down that had come loose when the birds squawked and jumped around to protest the intrusion of their living space by the pesky humans who lived downstairs. I rarely went into the Bird Room — I hated the smell and the noise and the unaffectionate nature of the birds — and instead focused my upstairs adventures on the room next door: an abandoned bathroom where spiders had long woven their webs from the faucet and around the nozzles of the sink and bathtub. It was by far the most interesting of these forsaken spaces. The tub was lined with long-dried bars of soap and rusty razors. I liked to sneak up there with a fork and steak knife and practice my cutting skills on old bars of Ivory soap. I hated the indignity of my mother cutting all my food for me. I figured I'd watch what my parents did at dinner, practice, and then surprise them one night when I could premiere my newfangled ability to cut my own food.

The third upstairs room was by all accounts the master bedroom; it was the largest in the house, but my parents had moved out of it when I was born, taking over a downstairs bedroom closer to my room. The only things that lived there now were a bed frame, a broken mirror, some newspapers from before I was born, and cat feces. It was the cleanest room in our house.

Our entire existence revolved around the kitchen, living room, and two bedrooms downstairs. The kitchen and living room took over half of the first floor and bled into one another, with the exception of a small aimless wall in the middle of the room. Against the dividing wall in the living room were a breakfront that housed porcelain Lladró figurines, dishes we never used, and an old black-and-white photograph of my mother. When I first discovered this photo, I asked why we had a picture of Aunt Lee naked and hiding behind a pillow. My mother and her sister looked so similar even I had a hard time telling them apart, the only real difference between them being that Lee was tall and my mother tiny. When my mother defensively announced that the sexy young woman in the photo was her, an obsession was born.

I couldn't imagine that my mother was ever the glamorous and coy woman looking back at me seductively while wearing nothing but a couch cushion. *My* mother wore her hair in a braid every day, had giant round glasses that dwarfed her skinny face and drank a glass of chocolate milk for breakfast every morning. *My* mother read *Madeline* in a French accent at bedtime and played my heavily scripted game of "mermaids" during bath time. The woman in the picture didn't seem like the kind of woman who would do those things, and I wanted to know everything about her. When no one was watching, I would climb atop the piles of yard sale finds and yellowing newspapers that took up the majority of the living room to get to that picture, so that I could inspect it tirelessly for signs of the mommy that I knew in the naked-pillow-wearing woman she once was.

There was a television in the living room, but because the three-seater brown couch with a tropical leaf pattern usually only had room for one adult at a time, most of our time spent as a family was spent on my parents' bed.

The kitchen was the room in the house that changed the most on a daily basis. At least, that is, the kitchen table. The table seemed to be in a constant state of flux between clean and piled high with my father's latest finds. My mother would indignantly tell my father that she wasn't going to clean up after him but would crack after a week or so of family meals at the foot of their bed, and the table would be cleared off for a few weeks before the stuff could take over again.

My bedroom was next to my parents'. My mother couldn't part with my crib when I outgrew it, and there was no room in the garage to store it, so it remained next to my twin-size bed. It became my de facto toy box; I would climb from my mattress over the wall of the crib to surround myself with the stuffed animals and dolls that made up the majority of my social life. At night, Cara, our German shepherd, would sleep under the crib. She had been doing it since my parents brought me home from the hospital.

My parents' bedroom was the center of life in our house. We ate our meals there on strategically placed folding tables when the kitchen became too messy. Their bed rested in the middle of the room, but both sides of the bed had become storage for the piles of old newspapers, worn and forgotten clothing, and must-have purchases that never needed to be had, trapping the beautiful antique armoires that once held neatly folded sweaters and carefully hung suits behind their mass. The surrounding trove only seemed to make the bed look bigger, as if it spread from wall to wall, the piles becoming makeshift closets and nightstands.

Inevitably I would wake up in the middle of the night, roused by my father's clamorous snoring, and stumble my way to their bedroom, where my mother would almost always already be awake to welcome me into a spot between her and my father.

My job was to wake my father up, so I would tap him on the head until his eyes opened.

"Why, hello there," was his usual answer.

To which I would reply, "Hello, you're snoring."

He would then roll over and the three of us would fall back to sleep.

"Are you mad at me?" I asked my mom when she put me to bed one night. We only had one more day to learn to be clean before our visitor came, and her exhaustion had taken a serious toll on her bedtime story enthusiasm.

"I'm not mad at you, I'm mad at what you did." This was my mother's standard-issue response, and this time I wasn't sure that I believed her. She was certainly mad at my father. After she turned my light off and closed my door, I heard the shouting start.

They had been fighting all week, but this was different; this time she sounded scared. "She's going to be taken away from us, is that what you want?" I heard her say. "You're going to lose your daughter because you can't get rid of a fucking newspaper."

My father didn't sound scared, he didn't sound like anything at all. He never answered my mother, at least not that I could hear from my bedroom. What I did hear was a door slam.

The house was silent until I woke up the next morning.

Each morning I would wake up amazed at the transformations that had happened while I was in bed, and each morning the barricade of black garbage bags in front of our home seemed to have grown exponentially.

I was excited for the social worker's visit. We had never had anyone to our house before, and I spent the morning anxiously dividing my time between standing in front of the door waiting to let him in and peeking out the front window for signs of incoming cars.

When the doorbell finally rang, I opened the door to a slim man with a bald head and gray moustache, wearing a short-sleeved button-down shirt. I introduced myself and invited him in. The house was cleaner than I had ever seen it, which only added to my excitement.

My parents introduced themselves and excused the remaining mess, and then my mom said, "Kim, why don't you go get Sheryl."

The previous night I had carefully planned out Sheryl's outfit. She would wear a purple and white corduroy dress that I had outgrown. The dress was too big for her, but it was my favorite. I carefully picked out a white undershirt for underneath the thin tie-straps. I didn't like when the cloth part of her body showed.

Sheryl was a gigantic Thumbelina doll. Unlike her thumb-sized literary namesake, Sheryl was two feet tall, only slightly shorter than I was when I started kindergarten, and until something better came along, she was my sister.

Earlier that day I had been anticipating this moment, but as I left my room I started to feel nervous. What if the social worker was mad at me? What if he took Sheryl away or took me to jail?

I made my way slowly down our now clean hallway and introduced the thin man with the short-sleeved shirt to my baby sister. When it became obvious that he wasn't going to take me to prison, I crawled up on his lap and asked if he would play hide-and-seek with me.

"You go hide, and when I'm finished talking to your parents, I'll come find you."

I loved hide-and-seek, but the only person who ever played it with me was my dad. He was terrible at finding me. I knew this because he would spend the majority of the game declaring aloud how baffled he was and what an "efficient absconder" I was. Eventually he would find me, though, and a new game of tag would ensue.

Since I had a new playmate to impress that day, I went to my favorite hiding place of all. In my bedroom there was a bookshelf, the bottom of which was always empty. When I wanted to go somewhere clean, I would curl up and lie there.

I must have fallen asleep, because when I woke up it was dark in my room. I crawled out, figuring it was about time to surrender my spot.

"Mommy, where's the man?"

My mother was in the kitchen making dinner. "He left."

"Did he even look for me?" I was hoping that my hiding spot was so good that he finally had to give up, but I had a sneaking suspicion that that was not the case.

"No, honey, he left a few minutes after you hid."

The fact that an adult would lie to me was painful. Sure, I lied all the time, but adults weren't supposed to lie. My parents never lied.

"It was good that you crawled up on his lap. If you were an abused child you wouldn't have done that," my mother told me.

I appreciated what I assumed was a compliment but was eager to get life back to normal. "Where's Daddy?"

"I don't know where your father is." This meant that they'd fought. I didn't know why. Aside from the CPS guy abandoning our game, I'd thought the day went pretty well. Which meant that my mom should have stopped yelling and my dad should have stopped storming off.

"We need to talk about something, Kim." My mom said. I was pretty sure that I was going to be in trouble. Usually when I did something bad, my mom would give me a countdown, but I would always acquiesce before she got to one. I wasn't sure what would happen at the end of the countdown, but I was pretty sure I didn't want to find out. This didn't seem to be that kind of trouble.

"Do you know what that man was doing here today?" My mom was always way calmer when I was in trouble than when Dad was.

"I lied and said Sheryl was my sister."

"Yes, and they believed you, which just goes to show that some people aren't too bright. Do you know why Daddy and I were so scared this week?"

I just shook my head. I had an idea, but I figured I'd wait for her to tell me in case I was wrong.

"Because our house is messier than other houses, and we

were afraid that the man who came here today would take you away from us."

My friends lived in clean houses; I lived in a dirty one. I'd always known we were different, but until now I didn't know that different was bad. Until now I hadn't known that there were people who could take me away from my parents. There was something wrong with us, and now that I knew it I couldn't unknow it. I loved my parents, and I loved my dogs, and my cats, and my panda, and my Sheryl, and I didn't want to leave any of them. My mom didn't have to finish the lecture.

"I won't tell anyone about Daddy."

FOUR

S HORTLY AFTER I was born, my father left the office job he shared with my mother and took a job driving a New York City bus.

"Everyone was so happy when your father got a job with the MTA," my mom told me. "He was such a nice guy that no one wanted to fire him, but his desk was piled so high with papers that he had to do his work on his lap."

I could picture that. I didn't understand exactly what my mom did, but I knew that she was the boss and that she "pushed papers." I imagined her with a shovel, shuttling piles of papers back and forth all day. I couldn't imagine my father being so harsh; he loved papers more than anything.

My mother left for work early in the morning, boarding a Manhattan-bound train before the sun came up. My dad left for his job later in the day after he had dropped me off at my babysitter, but on Thursdays and Fridays, otherwise known as Daddy Days, he was home to drive me to school. When he worked, he came home long after I had gone to bed, and my mom would wake me up in the middle of the night so that the three of us could steal a brief moment as a family. He'd pick me up and they would sandwich me between them. Because of my parents' incongruent work schedules, we were rarely together, and these family hugs were a nightly reminder that we were a team. Afterward my father would carry me back to bed and speed-read his way through a bedtime story, head-bobbing from exhaustion, before both of us fell asleep. He may not have been very good at bedtime, but he had morning wake-ups down to a science.

Step one: He would burst into my room, squealing, "Yoo-hoo, Mrs. Bloohooom!" in a high-pitched voice while flicking my light switch on and off.

If, and usually when, step one didn't succeed in rousing me out of bed, he would proceed to step two: singing *It's time to get up, it's time to get up, it's time to get up in the morning!* repeatedly while tickling me.

This usually worked, but I was proud, and would pretend to still be asleep while writhing around fending off his wiggly fingers.

Step three started with an additional five minutes of sleep, followed by him popping his head into my room over and over again, each time bellowing, "Y'up yet?"

If I wasn't up by the end of the triad, he'd steal my blankets and announce that I "better be up" by the time he got back. Neither of my parents was known for their disciplinary skills, but a serious tone was usually enough to scare me into good behavior.

Once I was up he was always a little unsure of what to do with me. Whenever he was in charge of feeding, hair-brushing, and clothing me, he'd generally ask my advice on how to operate the stove, use banana clips, or help me put on tights. For the most part he took my advice on how to raise me. And I was fully willing to use his parenting insecurities to my best interest.

"Mommy says I don't have to eat when Big Bird is on," I yelled back at my father after he beckoned me to the kitchen table to eat breakfast one day before kindergarten.

He lifted one eyebrow and grinned at me. My father always seemed to find humor in the things other grown-ups got mad about, like my constant lying.

"Somehow I doubt that, and you have to eat at the table." Faced with the reality that *Sesame Street* might be lost to me, I stayed firmly planted on the couch and started crying. My father was not one for saying no, nor was he one to interfere with anything deemed educational, which he had told me *Sesame Street* was. As I cried his focus faded from me. My father was prone to thinking spells — it was like someone turned off his switch, and he went from energetic playmate to reclusive overseer. He stood motionless for a moment, no longer looking at me but at a spot on the wall, and then turned and left, walking out the front door without so much as a good-bye. Confused, I stopped crying. I assumed my crying had made him so uncomfortable that he left.

He was gone for about ten minutes, long enough for me to worry that I'd been abandoned for bad behavior, but not so long that I would call my mom at work to tell on him. When he returned he was holding a pile of mirrors. He must have gone to the garage. I wasn't allowed to play in there, but I'd followed my dad before when he was looking for something, usually a tool of some sort. The garage was off-limits to anyone but my father because it was dangerous territory. There was no room to walk around. When tasked with finding something amid the piles of orderless tools, boxes, bags and tall mountains of newspapers, gears, paintings, clothes, and old things that smelled musty and spoiled, my father performed an intricate dance: lifting each leg high into the air and carefully placing it on a sturdy spot before attempting to hurdle over the piles with the other. Somewhere in the midst of the piles of forgotten stuff were those broken mirrors.

Without a word or a glance in my direction, he used the furniture separating our kitchen and living room as resting points for the mirrors and the books, magazines, newspapers, VHS tapes, and numerous tchotchkes that littered the living room to hold them in place.

"That should do it," he said, taking a step back to examine his work.

"Sit," he ordered.

He had aligned the mirrors in such a way that the image from the television reflected pinball machine style all the way through to the kitchen table.

Not only could I watch *Sesame Street*, but I could watch myself eating Cheerios while watching *Sesame Street*.

My father was the coolest person I knew, and I told him that. "Cool" was a new word I had learned from Jacob's older siblings, and I had decided it was the ultimate compliment one could get.

He beamed with pride at his new adjective.

"You know, when I was your age, I used to think that Howdy Doody lived in the television," he told me. "Do you know who Howdy Doody is?"

I had heard of Howdy Doody, probably from my father, but I didn't know who he was.

"*Howdy Doody* was my favorite show, and one day when no one was looking, I took apart the television with my father's tools to try and find him."

"Did you get in trouble?" I asked. The truth was, I thought the same thing about my favorite cartoon characters, but I never would have considered taking the television apart to find them. My mom would have been mad.

"I had to put the TV back together," he told me, and he laughed as if it was the first time he had ever heard the story.

My father, my mother told me, had almost no memory of his life before he was drafted into the army. He had blocked out most of his childhood, and the memories he did have he usually didn't share with me. I asked him endlessly what his parents had looked like, what they did, and if he thought they would like me, but each time he told me he couldn't remember and changed the subject. My mom told me that my dad's parents were alcoholics and were both long dead by the time she had met him, but she had heard stories of them over the years, some from my father, but most from other relatives. "It's better that he doesn't remember, Kim. Let him be."

When other daddies drank beer at barbeques or parties, my father stood alongside them holding a tan plastic Dunkin' Donuts mug filled with tea. I never saw him drink alcohol. He carried his own stash of tea bags with him and was, it seemed, on an endless search for hot water. When I first heard the word *teetotaler*, I thought it had been created just for him, a man who totes his tea.

I couldn't imagine my father as a boy my age. It was like he had started his life off as an adult.

"So, the Care Bears don't live in the TV?" I was waiting for the big reveal, but Daddy was lost in thought and never got to the point where he opened up his TV and Howdy Doody was standing there . . . or wasn't. Suddenly he was back, shaking off the memory like a mosquito. "Sorry, kiddo, the image of the Care Bears is transmitted through electromagnetic waves and then converted into viewable images by the technology inside the television."

"Do they live somewhere else?"

"You could say that." He smiled his big toothy smile. Daddy Days were fun.

Eventually we would have to leave. I was in an afternoon kindergarten session, so beforehand we would stop at a deli and he'd buy me a hard-boiled egg and a Capri Sun. We'd park by the water, throwing bits and pieces of stale bread to the ducks while we ate our lunch. My father always seemed to be genuinely interested in what I was thinking, not in the way adults often listen to kids with chuckles and feigned enthusiasm, but with genuine curiosity. On Daddy Days, my father would ask me what I was learning in school, discuss the news with me, and ask my opinion on the world I was growing up in.

My worldly knowledge was limited to our pets, my grandparents, and dance class, but I loved these talks and wanted nothing more than to impress him. I wanted him to think that I was as exciting as he was, so I'd make up stories, claiming to have swung from a trapeze during recess or saved a litter of kittens from the neighbor's dog.

He listened intently to every detail and asked me questions

about my adventures, helping me fill in the blanks where I lacked for ideas to make each story a bit more daring, somehow convincing me that they were all my own. I never doubted for a second that he believed me.

FIVE

VERY NIGHT BEFORE I went to sleep, I would con-
jure the image of the actor George Burns in my head and
ask him for the things I wanted most in life: new dolls, a
best friend, and for my house to burn down.

Religion was not a solidly formed concept for me, but I had
seen a movie about God once; he looked like George Burns and
was in the habit of causing trouble and granting wishes. I accepted him wholeheartedly as my savior.

My parents didn't talk about God. My mother was raised
vaguely Jewish, my father devoutly Catholic. They explained
each of their religious backgrounds to me like they explained
the countries their families had come from on heritage day at
school. Germans are orderly, Catholics believe in Jesus, Austri-
ans look like Germans only shorter, Jews had to put blood on
their doors so that George Burns wouldn't kill their firstborn
sons. We were people who ate matzo on Easter and ham on Ha-
nukah, and I was relatively sure that Christmas was somehow in-
tertwined with my birthday. It all made sense to me at the time.

I prayed for the same things every night, but each morning
I would wake up and I would have the same dolls I had gone

to bed with the night before (well, if I had a lost a tooth, the odds of having a new doll upon waking increased significantly); I was still lacking in friends, and my house was decidedly still standing.

Over the next two years, I continued to pray every night. The more I prayed, the messier the house got, but I knew that God was busy. There was a girl in my second grade class who had put her hand in a food processor when she was two years old; she had a thumb and part of her pinky finger left on that hand, but for the most part she had to do everything with her other hand. I thought she probably wouldn't mind living in a messy house if she could have her fingers back. And she probably ranked higher than I did on God's priority list.

My parents were rarely home, and yet the piles of junk and papers continued to fill each crevice of space, as if they moved in of their own accord. *Papers* is the generic term we used for my father's piles, because paper was by far the thing he collected most, but the piles that took over our home consisted of much more than paper. There was no rhyme or reason to what my father deemed important, and "paper" could consist of anything from an actual newspaper to a broken picture frame, tools, sweat-stained hats, or items that had fallen out of the pockets and purses of his bus passengers. These papers took over our dining room table again, and eventually the space that remained on the couch until the center of all family activity was relocated permanently to the foot of my parents' bed.

The fighting that had been sparked by the CPS man's visit years earlier had become the norm any time my parents were both home. Every fight was the same. My mother said she was tired of living in filth. She told my father that I would grow up to hate him. When he stormed off, as he usually did, without saying a word, I would pick up the fight. I would yell at her in return. If he wouldn't protect himself, I would protect him. *It wasn't that bad,* I told her. *I liked the way we lived,* I lied. *Daddy can't help it* was the only part of my argument that I knew was actually true. I knew that; I couldn't see why she didn't.

My parents were completely different outside the house. When we weren't home, we were normal. My parents sang along with the car radio and told me stories about their adventures pre-Kim, and my mother made a habit of tickling my father each time the car was stopped at a red light, relenting only when it turned green. My parents were always laughing as long as we weren't home.

I knew that if we could escape the papers we could be happy.

George Burns finally got around to me on February 14, 1989. It was a Wednesday, and I had woken up naturally, without tickling or blinking lights. My father was nowhere to be seen, and my first thought when I realized I had slept until 10 a.m. was that I would miss the Valentine's Day party my second grade class was throwing.

I rushed out of my room, ready to protest the loss of candy his tardiness had cost me, when I heard my mom. She should have been at work, but she was yelling at someone on the phone in her bedroom.

She looked up at me in her doorway just as she was slamming the phone down.

"Kimmy, what are we going to do with your father?" she said, motioning for me to sit on the bed next to her. She asked me that a lot, and I knew it didn't need answering.

"Your father was in an accident," she told me. "Part of the bus he was driving last night came loose and hit him on the head. He's hurt, but he'll live. He's driving home now."

I followed my mom to the kitchen and leaned against the refrigerator as she made me breakfast — toast with a hole in the shape of a heart, for Valentine's Day, with an egg cooked sunny-side up in the middle. As she cooked, she filled me in on the details of the accident. While driving, the Plexiglas visor in the front of his bus had swung loose, hitting him in the head once, then swung back to hit him again. When he started feeling dizzy and nauseous, he told his passengers that he was going express to the bus yard and drove himself to the nearest hospital. The doctors told him that he probably had a concussion. Since there was nothing but rest that could heal him, he decided to drive the two hours back to Long Island and rest at home.

I was more upset about not being on the receiving end of Valentine's Day cards and candy than I was about my father. I couldn't imagine that getting hit on the head by a visor would cause much damage.

I was wrong. When Daddy came home, he was different. What started as a day of sleeping in turned into weeks and then a month. There didn't seem to be enough rest in the world to make him better. My mother told me he was having migraines. He didn't want to watch TV or go to the pond anymore; he just wanted to be left alone. His moods were unreliable, and I never really knew which Daddy I was going to come home to. Sometimes he would get mad for no reason at all and punch his fist through a wall, and seconds later he would throw me over his shoulder and spin me around like he used to before the accident. More often, though, he seemed completely indifferent to everything and anyone.

Instead of working he would go to doctors' appointments. We were told that he had Post Traumatic Brain Injury Syndrome — which my mom said meant that the doctors had no idea why he hadn't fully recovered from the concussion. I had the feeling he wasn't really sick anymore, but that he'd finally wandered off like I had always been afraid of; his body just hadn't gone anywhere.

I didn't think much of it when my mother announced at the end of April that we would be moving to the Bronx, just the two of us, to take care of my grandmother. Grandma had developed gangrene in her foot, which my mother informed me meant that her foot was rotting, and we needed to clean it regularly so that she wouldn't have to get it cut off.

I learned years later from my aunt Lee that my mother's story was only partly true. My grandmother did have gangrene in her foot, but her ailment coincided with yet another visit from CPS. This time there was no mistake — they were not called about the unfair treatment of dolls in our household. A neighbor had reported the conditions of our house. The mess was worse than it had ever been — our beds, toilet, and tub had become the only visible surfaces left — and my father didn't want to do anything but sleep. Faced with the fact that she couldn't clean the house alone, my mother had decided to leave my father for good. She fled to my grandmother's apartment and enrolled me in a new school district so that I wouldn't be taken away from her.

SIX

THE SMELL OF OLD APARTMENT buildings and
their aged wood and dusty railings marked a welcome
change to my surroundings. I loved everything about
the Bronx and couldn't understand why my parents would ever
trade in the hustle and bustle of city life for Long Island.

The walls of my grandparents' apartment were lined with
old family photographs: baby pictures of my grandfather that
I thought were funny because he was wearing a dress, and old
photos of people who had died long before I was born, taken in
countries I had never given much thought to. My favorite pictures were my grandparents' wedding photos. My grandmother
had been the great beauty of our family: alabaster skin, thick
black hair that had always been worn in a bob just above her
shoulders, and a round face that made her look like a real-life
version of Snow White. My grandfather was tall and skinny, his
olive skin tone and dark hair making him look more Italian than
Jewish. He looked nothing like the blind, round-bellied, pale
man that I had known.

My grandfather had died a few months earlier. When he was
alive, he would sing me Louis Armstrong songs while teaching

me to cook. He told me, "If a starfish cuts off a finger it will grow back, but you are not a starfish, and you have to be very careful with knives because your fingers won't grow back."

Taking care of Grandma's foot should have been his job.

There weren't many pictures of my mom on the wall of pictures, which I always felt slightly cheated by. This seemed to only support my mother's argument that her parents never particularly cared much for her, a fact that I had adamantly decided not to accept. Whenever the opportunity arose I attempted to pester my mom into liking Grandma, and Grandma into saying nice things about my mom. It seemed beyond my understanding that a mother and a daughter could not love one another. Parents love their kids, kids love their parents — that seemed like a universal truth. But according to my mom, it didn't always work that way.

My mother was left alone for most of her childhood: She remembers being handed a box of cereal and told to watch TV and not bother anyone, or being kicked out of the house to go play in the street when she was barely out of diapers. When she broke her collarbone on the way to school when she was five, she listened to the school nurse berate my grandmother for not deeming it important to come pick her daughter up and take her to a doctor. Grandma told the nurse my mom could walk home after school and she would deal with the problem then.

But the biggest area of neglect in my mother's upbringing was her back. During a routine doctor visit when she was seven years old, the family doctor informed my grandparents that their daughter had already started to show strong curvatures in her spine. In order to lead a normal life, they were told, my mother would need to be fitted for a back brace immediately to help contain her scoliosis while her tiny body grew.

They refused. My mother grew up, but not much. Her S-shaped spine, if stretched out, would have her measure at five feet, eight inches, the same height as her nearly identical younger sister. Instead she is four foot nine.

As a result of her curved spine, my grandfather would tell her during her teenage years that "No decent man will ever want you." She set out to prove him right, dating one bad boy after another, even marrying one at eighteen just to get of the house. Her ill-fated first marriage was annulled within a year — more proof for her family that she was a screw-up.

My grandparents' apartment wasn't tidy by any stretch of the imagination, but it was less messy than our house, and therefore clean by default. I slept in the room my mom had shared with my aunt until she left home, and my mom slept on the couch in the living room. There was a third bedroom in the apartment, but it was full to the brim with things no one used. It didn't strike me as odd that my grandparents had a junk room. There were plenty of rooms in our house we didn't use.

Despite the cool climate between her and my mother, I liked Grandma. She read the newspaper to me every day. One day she read me the story of a girl my age who had fallen down an elevator shaft not far from where Grandma lived and had died. I made her read the story to me over and over again.

"Do you enjoy this?" My grandmother asked me.

"No." I did though. I was fascinated by the idea that someone my age could die, but I didn't want to tell her that. I liked our daily newspaper reading, and I didn't want her to stop. I was used to hearing the news on the radio and loved having it told to me like a story, curled up against her on her bed.

At lunchtime she would make us peanut butter and jelly sandwiches on cinnamon raisin bread. PB&J was a favorite food of hers, but neither of her children had liked it, so my grandmother had waited until she was well into her sixties to have someone in the family to share it with. Unlike my mom, Grandma always wore lipstick — bright reds or pinks that smelled waxy and accentuated the contrast between her dark hair and pale skin. She called me "my darling" and made me a cradle for my Glow Worm in an arts and crafts class.

I decided to give my grandmother the benefit of the doubt and chalk my mom's feelings up to a big misunderstanding.

"Do you love my mom?" I asked my grandmother one day after school.

"Yes. Why would you ask that?" Grandma didn't seem so much shocked by my question as she was suspicious that I was accusing her of something.

"I don't think Mommy knows. Maybe you should tell her," I suggested. "Maybe you could hug her."

"I'll talk to her about it," she said, proceeding to change the subject by averting her attention back to the episode of *Father Dowling Mysteries* we were watching.

I was pretty sure I'd just mended all fences between the two maternal figures in my life. I patted myself on the back as Grandma and I watched our favorite mystery-solving priest together.

The talk they had later consisted of more yelling than talking.

"That child is the only thing you've ever done right!" I heard her yell from her bedroom.

My mother said something about Grandma being an ungrateful old witch, and then —

"I should have just let you rot," she said as she slammed Grandma's bedroom door and came to find me in the living room.

"Kim, there are some things you don't repeat!"

"It wasn't a lie."

"No, it wasn't a lie. But we don't have to talk about everything that's true."

"I'm sorry." I apologized because I'd obviously done something wrong, but I was angry. I was getting increasingly confused about what was okay to discuss in my life.

My mom was exasperated. "It's okay. She was right. You are the only thing I've ever done right."

The kids were different in Grandma's neighborhood. They seemed to be a little bit older than their seven or eight years. I was one of only two white kids in my class, a stark difference from my almost exclusively white classmates on Long Island. It never occurred to me that I didn't fit in, and I felt the salutation of "new white girl" was as apt a description as any. There were no carpools or play dates to dodge — kids walked home after school and played with whomever they could find loitering the hallways of their building. During lunch they traded war stories in the cafeteria, stories about mothers leaving them with their grandparents and not coming back or cousins who had been killed. I didn't talk about my dad because I had promised not to, and I doubted many of my classmates would understand what it was like to have too much, but for the first time my secret felt like a good thing. I fit in with these kids and their unfair lives.

The climate between my mother and my grandmother neither improved nor worsened after my botched effort to make us one big happy family. Their relationship was what it had always been: an obligation neither was particularly grateful for. I finally understood what my mother had been trying to explain: She didn't feel about Grandma the way I felt about her, and Grandma didn't love my mom the way my mom loved me.

My mother continued to clean and bandage Grandma's gangrene until my father called one night at the end of June. I was already in bed, but my mom woke me up, brushing the hair from my face. She was much gentler in her wake-ups than Dad was, but also less effective.

"Kim, honey, I need you to get up," she whispered.

I sat up in bed. The room was still dark, but the light from the hallway illuminated enough of the room for me to see her sitting on my bed.

"Daddy just called."

I was still groggy and it took me a while to realize what my mother was trying to tell me. "There was a fire," she said.

I hadn't prayed in months. I hadn't asked God to burn down our house since we had moved in with Grandma. A part of me hoped we might stay with Grandma and that my father could visit a few days a week so we could live here indefinitely.

"Daddy's okay," she said. My father was asleep in the bedroom when it happened, and had to climb out a window to escape. My dogs had died, and our cats, and all of the birds in the Bird Room. Misty was going to have kittens — I was sad about that, but mostly I was mad at myself . . . God had gotten it all wrong. He wasn't supposed to kill my pets. I should have been more specific.

My mom and I stayed up all night. I cried, she didn't. She had nothing to feel guilty about.

My dad showed up in the early hours of the morning. As soon as I heard his keys in the door, I ran and waited for it to open, and he immediately picked me up.

"Hey, kiddo, shouldn't you be sleeping?" My dad seemed almost normal again, and I thought that maybe his migraines burned up in the house, too.

"Can't. I'm sad."

"Well at least rest a bit then." With that, he carried me back to my temporary bedroom and tucked me back into bed, where I promptly fell asleep.

When I woke up, Ebony, our black cocker spaniel puppy, was in bed with me. She had been in the bedroom with my dad when the fire started — she was the only one he could save. When she was an even smaller puppy and we still lived at home, I used to come home every day from school and read *Bingo* to her; it was the only book I had about a dog.

Not only had the fire killed my pets, but I would miss my last day of school because of it. Instead of the field trip I was supposed to go on to celebrate the year's end, my parents and I packed up our puppy and headed back to what was left of the house to meet with someone from the insurance company. The two-plus-hour trip back to the suburbs was mostly silent. There was nothing to say, except the obvious.

"Do you believe in God?" I asked.

Mom said she didn't believe in God because there were children dying in Africa. "There are a lot of terrible things in this world, and I can't believe in a god that would allow innocent children to starve to death," she told me.

That wasn't the answer I was looking for, so I waited for my father's response. He knew pretty much everything, so I was positive he would know whether God was real or not. "I haven't seen any convincing empirical evidence that would either confirm or deny the existence of God," he told me, his eyes fixed on the road ahead.

I wanted to tell them that I knew the truth, that there was a God and I had proof. God had answered my prayer. But if I told them, they would think I was bad. I had wished for our house to burn down, and it did. I just wanted a new house, a clean house, a house that wasn't full of paper, and then we could be normal and I could have sleepovers.

All of this talk about spirituality set my father off on a rant about transcendentalism. This wasn't the first time in my life that I'd been roped into a discussion pertaining to Walden Pond, so I let him talk, *uh-huh*-ing periodically, while my mind wandered.

Up until this point, I had considered God to be some sort of benevolent genie. If you prayed the right way, your wish would be granted. I had wished for something bad to happen, and it had. But I couldn't help but think my mom was right: There were kids in this world that had it a lot worse off than I did, and I was sure they prayed, too. So why hadn't God listened to them, but had instead listened to me?

When my father's rant on the innate goodness of man ended,

the car again became silent, which was good because I still had questions I wanted answers to.

"Daddy, did you cry?"

"No, kiddo, I didn't cry. But that doesn't mean I'm not sad."

"Mommy, did you cry?"

My mom didn't answer. My father's monologue had given her the perfect opportunity to pretend to be sleeping. I could tell she wasn't really napping, since I could see her reflection in the mirror and her mouth was closed. When my mother was really asleep her head flopped to the side and her mouth hung open.

I didn't want to be responsible for my parents crying. This was my fault. I had burned down the house. I had killed all our animals. I should have been more specific when I prayed, I should have told God not to let our pets die.

SEVEN

THE HOUSE LOOKED DIFFERENT than I expected it to. In my mind, I had imagined a conelike pile of ashes, the way it happened in cartoons. It had "burned down," after all, so I expected it to be down, but the house I had prayed so hard to destroy was still standing. The fire had started in the walls of the kitchen, toward the back of the house, and there was nothing left there but the charred remains of appliances.

My bedroom had completely imploded, taking a good portion of the upstairs we never used with it. "It was a good thing you were at Grandma's," my mom said. The kitchen was gone, as was the garage, but there were still parts of my parents' room that were left unscathed.

I was ordered to sit in the car while my parents spoke with the insurance adjuster, Bruno. Mom said she didn't want me breathing in the soot, but I could smell the sour smoky twinge to the air from inside the car. I stayed with Ebony and decided to search for whatever treasures I could find in the backseat. My dad always kept bags of papers in the car, lots of them. Every time we went to the car, there was a fight about it, and in order to keep the arguing to a minimum, I would often tell him to clean the car out before we left to go somewhere, or I would go out and clean it up myself when he seemed particularly distracted. The trunk was always full to the brim with paper, too, so it was better to let him do it — Dad had a way of making it all fit somehow.

Since my father had been on his own for months, no one had forced him to clean out the car, and so I rummaged through the ample bags looking for entertainment. Sometimes there was candy mixed in with the newspapers, old lottery tickets, receipts, weathered paperbacks, and store flyers. If I was lucky, I'd find a Kit Kat.

Periodically, I would stop my search and see what the grown-ups were doing. Bruno was the biggest man I'd ever seen. He was far taller than my father and also much heavier. He had a round nose and loose hairs that he combed over his bald head. He reminded me of Wimpy from Popeye, only if Wimpy were the size of Andre the Giant.

I watched the grown-ups talk and shake hands while consoling Ebony. I was sure she was sad; her mother, Merry, had died in the fire. If I found a candy bar, I would give her half.

When Bruno left, my mom came back to the car to sit with me while my dad poked around the wreckage that was once their bedroom. A while later he emerged, reeking of smoke and covered in ash but holding two mostly intact picture frames that had been in my parents' bedroom. They were baby pictures of me, the only pictures that had survived. That's when my mother's tears came. Silently. She didn't sniffle and wail the way I did when I cried, but I could see the reflection of her wiping away tears in the visor mirror.

I watched her reflection the entire ride back to Grandma's house. I didn't ask any more questions.

When we returned to the Bronx, our belongings were in boxes in the hallway and the locks had been changed. My mother banged on the door, but all she heard from her mother was that she didn't want us leeching off of her.

That was the last time I saw my grandmother. But I didn't know that yet. All I knew then was that we were all together again, and that we were homeless.

We slept in the car that night. The next day, my mother arranged for the insurance company to put us up at a hotel. We drove back to Long Island and moved into the Comfort Inn. The only other time I had slept in a hotel was when we went to Disney World when I was four.

I loved everything about our hotel home. We were strategically located next to a 7-Eleven and had an inground swimming pool at our disposal. On the days that my mom had to work, I would usurp the pool as my own personal playground and bestow the honor of babysitting me to whichever lifeguard was on duty. When I got tired and pruny, I would pester my dad to walk the thirty feet to the 7-Eleven with me. Slurpees and chlorine became the staples of my diet that summer.

Normally I wasn't allowed to have big sugary drinks, but I had overheard my mom tell people that I was traumatized — which somehow meant I was allowed to eat candy and swim all day. I didn't feel traumatized, but if it meant a daily bout of brain freeze I was all for playing up my sadness.

I overheard a lot that summer, making it my business to listen in on as many grown-up conversations as I could, trying to piece together what life meant for our family now.

I took a lot of bathroom breaks when we visited my friend Jacob and his parents. Their bathroom was next to the kitchen, where the parents would sit and talk while we played. With my ear to the door, I heard Jacob's dad, Mike, say, "It was an electrical fire. It could have happened to anyone."

"If it was your house, it wouldn't have happened," my dad responded. I only heard three voices after that: June's, Jacob's mother; Mike's; and my mom's.

A hand-washing later, I left my eavesdropping station to go find my dad. It didn't take much looking on my part; he was where he always was: in the car, driver's side door open, one foot in and one out, drinking tea and listening to the radio. I took over the passenger seat.

"How're you holding up?" he asked me.

"I'm okay. How are you holding up?"

"I'm okay, too."

And with that established, we sat in the car together listening to NPR.

EIGHT

THE SUMMER WAS A WHIRLWIND of house hunting and yard sale-ing. Shopping for real estate became my new favorite hobby. It was like playing the biggest game of pretend ever; within ten minutes of stepping into a potential house, I lived a thousand lives. I could imagine myself sitting on the floor playing board games on soft carpets — something I'd never been able to do in our last house. I thought about bubble baths in tubs with Jacuzzi jets and rooms just for my toys. I spent hours studying the JC Penney catalog, picking out canopy beds with pink accessories or wicker daybeds with burgundy shams. I carried the catalog with me wherever we went, comparing my fantasy life with available real estate. In these houses, I had the most perfect, most tidy, most normal of lives.

Inevitably we'd end up at a yard sale after our days of house browsing, and all those daydreams shattered. We didn't have a house yet, but that didn't stop us from buying the things that other people didn't want anymore: a waffle maker, given as a wedding gift to a couple we didn't know; a coffee table that might match a couch we didn't own; and numerous other doo-dads we might be able to piece a life around.

I hated yard sales. To me, used stuff was junk, and we had just gotten rid of all of our junk. Our hotel room began to look more and more like our house had. Each new purchase recreated the claustrophobic conditions I'd prayed so hard to get away from. The hotel was starting to feel like home.

After a month, the insurance company stopped paying for our hotel. According to them, we needed to make a choice: re-build, which would consist of living in a trailer on our front yard, or buy a new house. My mom couldn't stomach the idea of living in front of the wreckage, so we downgraded to an hourly-rate motel off of the highway willing to give us a discount. Cheap and small and dingy, there was no pool or almond-scented shampoo, but for the time being it would suffice as home. Unlike the Com-fort Inn, the maids at the motel would come tidy up the room whether we were in it or not, which meant I got to spend a lot more face time with the cleaning staff.

I was fascinated by the women who would come in and out of each room with carts of toilet paper, towels, and Lysol. At first I would just watch them attentively, but as I got more comfort-able, I started following them around to other rooms, watch-ing the way they made tight corners with the sheets and wiped down any visible surfaces with dingy rags.

Most didn't speak much English, or at least pretended not to, and therefore couldn't tell me to get lost. The exception was Rosa, who was younger than the other maids and made a habit of winking at me each time I passed her and her cart of towels on the way to the ice machine. I made up a story that she was the daughter of the hotel's owner, the owner decidedly being the man in the office who gave out the room keys. When she came to clean our room, I perched myself on the faux-wood-finished dresser that furnished the barebones hotel room and watched her every move.

"Hi. I like the way you make the beds," I told her.

"I can show you how, if you want," she responded, and waved me over to her.

I'm not sure where my father was at this point. I assumed he was sitting in the car listening to the radio, and I hoped he wouldn't come back and ruin my opportunity to get a house-keeping tutorial from a real-life maid. Rosa taught me how to make tight corners with top sheets and creases for the pillows and how to properly fold the bedspread. The next day, I had the beds made before she got there, but she allowed me to follow her into the empty guest rooms and make them up.

If Rosa was annoyed by my overzealous companionship, she didn't show it, and she let me help with the dusting, polishing, and vacuuming — things I had never done or seen my parents do at home. My favorite chore remained bed-making, but I made careful mental notes about each housekeeping duty we did together so that I would have a plan of action for my family's new house. I would take over the cleaning in our new house, and I would ask my parents to give me an allowance. I had seen that on TV.

My parents' goal was to move before the school year started in September, since I couldn't register for school from a hotel. As August approached, my mom took more and more time off of work to dedicate to our hunt for a new home. The prospect of finding, closing, and moving into a house in less than a month seemed increasingly unlikely. Especially given my mother's propensity to hate every house she saw.

My dad didn't have much of an opinion about where we ended up, but my mother found veto reasons in white carpets, narrow doorways, shower doors, lack of fencing, and floral wallpaper. There didn't appear to be a house on Long Island that was right for our family.

And then we saw the worst of the lot: tan and brown on the outside, orange shag carpet on the inside, overgrown shrubbery, and a guest bathroom decorated with pea-green reflective wallpaper. In my eyes, there was absolutely nothing right with this place, but my mother was in love. It didn't hurt that the owner of the two-story, four-bedroom, three-bathroom house, with a two-car garage and an attic that was so big the real estate agent said that we could convert it into an apartment, had already bought a new home in Florida and was looking to close immediately.

Whether I liked it or not, we were going to have a new house. A big house, far bigger than our family of three needed. I was determined to look on the bright side. The only redeeming value I could assign the house was its sheer magnitude. I was sure there was no way my dad would be able to find enough paper to fill it all up.

We moved in a couple of weeks later and paid cash for the house, thanks to the payout from the insurance company. Our first night at the house, I unwrapped the new broom and mop that my parents had bought that day, and, true to my promise, I started on chores. They were pretty easy, seeing as how there was no furniture yet. I swept and mopped our newly acquired kitchen while my parents brought in the few belongings we'd had at Grandma's and those we'd been stockpiling in our hotel rooms.

"Daddy, you're not going to make this house messy, right?"

"I'll try, kiddo." My dad didn't like to make promises he couldn't keep.

NINE

I BELIEVED THAT I COULD rewrite everything about myself after the fire. Third grade started shortly after we moved in, and everything in my life was new: I had new clothes, new shoes, new dolls, a new book bag, and a new house to have friends over to — all I needed was new friends.

I had the fresh start I always wanted, but I was still me. Still shy and barely audible in the presence of anyone my own age, still hyper and gregarious around anyone over thirty. When school started, I was teased for being shy and for being new, and for anything else I dared to be. Being awkward wasn't new to me, but being teased for it was. When I would come home crying after school, my parents implored me to defend myself. My father taught me the correct way to throw a punch, but told me never to hit anyone unless I thought they were going to hit me first.

"You just need to put one bully in their place, and the rest will stop," my mom said. But being a kid wasn't quite as cut-and-dried as she thought. When I tried to stand up for myself, I was teased more, and so I stayed quiet.

I dreaded gym class. I wasn't particularly athletic, but that wasn't the reason I hated this quasi-free period. During our other classes, everyone had to be quiet, and so I had a reprieve from teasing. But in gym, the kids could talk, so they were free to make fun of me. When our gym teacher lined us up against the wall and told us to run the length of the gym while he threw a football our way to catch, I prayed that I might actually catch it.

I'd never played football. I'd never seen a football. I had no idea how to catch a football, but miraculously the first one sent my way found its way into my hands.

Despite my uncharacteristic athletic prowess, there was no amnesty from teasing by the boys in my class. I still said nothing.

"I would shut up, John, she's doing better than you are," the girl next to me said when I got back in line. Her name was Carolynn, and she'd never even glanced in my direction before. I smiled. That was as much of a thanks as I could muster, but she stood with me in line as we walked back to class.

"Do you play soccer?" she asked.

"I've played a few times," I lied. I'd never played soccer, but that was just a technicality.

"My dad coaches the Knight Copiers, you should join the team."

I told my parents that night over dinner that I loved soccer and wanted to join Carolynn's team. They looked at me like an alien life form that had invaded their avoid-other-children-at-all-costs daughter, but the next day my mom made the appropriate phone calls. By the following weekend, I had a purple and black uniform, shin guards, and cleats, and my parents had a bag full of sliced oranges to bring to my first-ever soccer game. I was immediately assigned my position as a left forward, but having no idea what that meant, I just ran up and down the soccer field, staying parallel to the ball as Carolynn's father had told me to.

I hoped that if perchance the ball ever got anywhere near me, someone else would come and kick it before I had to. I didn't know which goal belonged to my team.

A soccer phenom I was not, but thanks to weekly practices and games, I was becoming better and better friends with Carolynn. After going to her house for playdates a few times, I did something I had never done before — I reciprocated.

We didn't have much yet — a couch, a recliner, beds, a dining room table. I didn't care if we ever got more furniture; I loved living in a big empty house. Well, almost empty. In the front foyer there was a closet with brown accordion-style doors, and inside my father had started hiding bags of papers. Free local papers that he picked up each time we went to the grocery store, flyers from local discount stores, and real estate brochures he had collected during our house-hunt but wasn't quite ready to let go of. On the shelves lining the walls of the closet, he kept tools and extra portable radios so that he could carry the news with him wherever he went.

The day before Carolynn came over, I made plans for things we could do together. I brushed all my dolls' hair and lined them up on my daybed. My big white orangutan, Sugar, was on one side, with the rest of my dolls arranged in a lineup that progressed size-wise from Melissa my Magic Nursery Baby and eventually to my nameless Barbies.

My father had grown progressively more distant since we moved in. While living in a big clean house enlivened my mother and me, it seemed to have the exact opposite effect on my father. He still wasn't working, but he wasn't lying in bed with migraines anymore either. Mostly he sat in the car or his room listening to the radio and reading whatever newspaper or book he had hidden from my mother's sight. I woke up for school on my own, thanks to an alarm clock, and he came out from hiding in time to pick my mother up at the train station each night. We still had dinner together at night, at a clear table, and sometimes he could be coerced to be himself for a few minutes and forget that everything he loved had been taken from him.

He was expectedly absent when Carolynn arrived for our play date. She had only been over a few minutes and I was still giving her the tour of our house when my dad stormed into the living room.

His face was purple and he was yelling at me. I couldn't understand what he was saying — the words were jumbled as he spat them at me. He was calling me a brat, I understood that much.

"All I want is to listen to the news," he said.

Then there was some more yelling about a broken radio, and I figured it out. He thought I had broken his radio, but I didn't know which radio he was talking about — there were radios strategically placed all over the house so that a moment of NPR would never be missed. His tirade included the word "closet," and so I guessed that a radio must have fallen off a shelf and broken. I hadn't broken it. I tried to tell him that, but he just kept yelling. I thought about "The Boy Who Cried Wolf." My mom used to tell me that story all the time during my lying phase, and it seemed that I was in my own version; he wasn't hearing any of my pleas of innocence. He wasn't looking at me. He didn't appear to be looking anywhere at all, completely unfocused in his rage.

When he taught me how to make a fist to fight off bullies, he had said, "Make sure your thumb is outside, so that you don't break it." And just like he had instructed me, he made a fist, and he punched me in the face. And then, with that same unfocused look in his eyes, he walked out of the room.

I wasn't going to hit him first.

My face was throbbing, but I was too shocked by what had happened to cry.

"I think I want to go home now," Carolynn said. "I'm scared of your dad."

I was torn between telling her that my dad wasn't usually like this, that my parents never hit me, or acting like this sort of thing was no big deal and happened all the time. Instead, I walked her to the kitchen phone where she called her mom to come pick her up. When she was done, we waited outside in the driveway. We didn't speak. There was nothing to say.

By then I knew that I didn't have to talk about everything that was true, especially if it meant someone was going to get in trouble, so I didn't tell my mom about what had happened in front of Carolynn. My father would get in trouble, and he'd been in a lot of trouble lately.

By the time we'd been in the new house for almost a year, the bags of papers that my father had been hiding in closets, cabinets, drawers, and the garage started to make their way into the open. Hiding their existence made them easier to ignore. I didn't want to admit that my dad was doing the same thing here that he'd done to our old house, and I don't think that my mother did either.

This was her dream home. I still couldn't see why and still hated this house, but my mother assured me that she wanted to change all the things about it that I disliked anyway. One day, she promised, this house would be beautiful. There were constant talks of taking down the tacky green and silver wallpaper in the bathroom, painting rooms and changing carpets, but none of that ever happened, and so we were stuck with rusty-orange carpets and black art deco furniture, a theme that made our downstairs resemble a constant ode to Halloween.

By the time the school year ended, my parents were fighting like they had in the old house, more so because this time there was something at stake: our chance to be normal. The worst fight of all happened in July. We didn't have air-conditioners yet, and my uniform around the house consisted of white cotton undershirts and underpants. I was in my room when the yelling started, playing with the new stereo system my parents had bought me at a yard sale. I couldn't raise the volume enough to drown out my mother's voice.

She was screaming, "I'm not going to let you do this to another house." She had found his stash, bags and bags of things, when they came tumbling out of the hall closet. And he had already filled most of the two-car garage.

I thought about the homeless man when my parents fought. As broken as my father was, he was still my responsibility to protect. I left the confines of my room and ran down the stairs to interject.

By the time I got downstairs it was too late — he was gone. He never responded to my mother's arguments with more than a stream of mumbles, but he could slam the door so that the whole house shook. The car was still in the driveway, which meant wherever he was he was on foot, and so I started screaming.

I wanted him to hear me and come back.

My mother didn't ask me to stop screaming. My allegiance was with my father, I had proven that fight after fight, and so she left me to scream myself out at the foot of the stairs. I screamed for an hour, maybe more. Wherever my father was at this point, he probably couldn't hear me, but I kept going even though my face and throat ached.

Echoes of "Daddy" carried down the street until a neighbor's boyfriend knocked on our door and asked my mother if he could come inside. The neighbors thought I was being beaten and had elected him to find out. He told my mother he would call the police if she didn't allow him to confirm my safety.

The intrusion to my hysterics finally quieted me. My mother, far more collected than she had been when screaming at my father, assured him that I was only having a tantrum, but eventually acquiesced and allowed this stranger to inspect my body for lesions.

In my undershirt and underpants, I looked at her nervously when the neighbor asked for me to lift the back of my shirt so that he could look me over for marks. My mother just nodded her head at me, as if to say, *Don't look at me, you did this to yourself.*

"I just had to check," he told my mother as he left.

"Are you embarrassed?" She asked as she shut the door behind him.

I nodded my head yes.

"So am I." It was clear that my father was not the only one that she was angry at. I had humiliated her just like my father did.

· · ·

I wasn't afraid of my parents divorcing. I was afraid of what would happen to my father without my mother. He needed her — probably more than I did. I was afraid that without her to anchor him to a normal life he would be just as content to live in boxes or subway stations . . . to live without me.

Wherever my father was that night, he stayed there until after I had gone to bed. I had left the door to my bedroom open, hoping I'd wake up when he climbed up the stairs, but all the screaming had worn me out and I slept right through his middle-of-the-night homecoming. When I woke up the next morning, he was home and sitting on the edge of my mother's bed, as if nothing had ever happened.

Shortly after we moved into the new house, my parents stopped sharing a bedroom. My father took over the guest room, where he slept on a trundle bed. Because of his piles of paper, the trundle bed could only half extend. He slept on that lower bed, with papers on the floor piled to upper-mattress level and surrounding him on all sides. The upper mattress became a desk of sorts, with its own stash of newspapers, catalogs, and documents preserved above the tides of trash.

My mother stayed in the master bedroom, and checking in with her was my first stop each morning.

"Morning, honey. Come sit down," my mom said. She seemed far more upbeat than was normal for a postfight morning.

"Your father is going away for awhile," she said, indicating that it was my father's job to deliver this news.

I looked at him, thinking of all the possible places he might be going — back to the hotel, Grandma's apartment, wherever he had been the night before. None seemed like a likely choice.

"Where?"

He looked down at his clasped hands, rubbing his thumbs together. "I'm going to the funny farm." He reached over to tickle me, not being one for tense moments. "Should be funny," he said, and I laughed, because I couldn't help it, but I knew it wasn't funny.

When he stopped, I jumped to my feet. "Hold on," I said, and ran to my room to grab my school picture.

"Will you keep this in your room?" I said, holding out the picture as I ran back to him.

He looked at it and smiled, and looked over at my mother. "Why, of course. I'll be the envy of all the other crazy daddies."

TEN

FTER MY FATHER LEFT for the mental hospital, I moved into my mother's room. I set up shop on the side of the bed that was once intended to be my father's.

I was a little too old to be sleeping in my parents' bed, but my mother accepted my recent clinginess as a phase and never told me I had to leave. I was also too old for bedtime stories, but I told them to myself anyway. My most comforting fantasy starred my anatomically correct doll, Susan. She had an anatomically correct brother, Jerome, and my parents had used them both to teach me about the differences between boys and girls after I stumbled upon some inappropriate cable channels years earlier and told my class that boys had tails that they put in girls. I held Susan close to me, pretending I was her mother and that we were homeless.

In my story, I was a down-on-her luck mother living under a highway overpass with her infant daughter. It wasn't hard to imagine. From mattress to wall, there was a solid bevy of stuff, newspapers and magazines that engulfed clothes and shoes and boxes and toys — they were the worn tires, cardboard boxes, and general debris that I imagined found its home under a bridge. I promised Susan that I would find her someplace nice to live, and fell asleep each night singing her the lullabies my mother had sung to me.

I didn't return to my own room when my father came home from the inpatient psychiatric facility a week after he left.

He had called my uncle Aaron, who was actually a friend of my mother's from work, to pick him up and drive him home. My father never went anywhere without his gigantic key ring, but he rang the bell nonetheless and waited for me to answer it. We had stopped letting people into the house by this point, so I started to open the door the way I always had: just enough so that I could see the person standing in front of it, without them being able to get a real look inside. But when I saw that it was my father, I was so happy to see that he was home that I let the door swing open behind me so I could jump into his arms.

"Hey, kiddo," he said as he picked me up. I started crying, overwhelmed by the fact that he was home and he was fixed.

My mom rushed outside, closing the door behind her to keep Aaron from seeing in. She and Aaron stood on the front lawn talking while my father and I went inside and got reacquainted with the house. I followed him as he made his way upstairs and to his bedroom.

"Wanna grab me a garbage bag?" he said, and I rushed downstairs to find the garbage bags on the mass of things that lived on the kitchen table.

We sat next to one another on the lower mattress in his bedroom, sorting papers. He examined each scrap of paper I handed him, scouring it for whatever it was that had made him think it was important enough to keep in the first place. Things were put in two piles: treasures and trash.

"What was it like?" I asked him, handing him a brochure so he could decide its fate.

"It was like a hotel full of crazy people."

"What did you do?" I had never known anyone who had gone to a mental hospital before, and I imagined that they put my father in a straitjacket and used electroshock therapy. That's what I had seen on TV.

"Group therapy, mostly."

"What did you talk about?" Assembly line–style questioning of my father was nothing new for me. I could listen to my father talk about nothing and everything for hours. It didn't matter what the question I asked him was, the answer would inevitably take twists and turns through world politics, linguistics, poetry, and architecture, but getting him to tell me anything about himself required time and patience and a whole lot of pointed questions. In general, I was grateful for whatever nugget of personal insight he could spare, but this time I wanted a specific answer. I wanted him to say that he talked about me, that he wanted to be clean for me, and that I mattered more to him than all of his papers.

"Nothing," he said. "I didn't have much to say."

His garbage bag wasn't even a quarter full by the end of his first day home, and at the speed my father was going he would have the floor of his room clean in just under a thousand years. But he was trying, and that was enough for me.

I wanted my mother to be as excited to have my father back as I was, but she told me not to get my hopes up. The doctors had diagnosed him as depressed with ADD — attention deficit disorder. "Your father is the least depressed person I have ever met," she said. The doctors didn't know why my father loved everything in the world so much that he had to live with it all, so they gave him a prescription for Prozac and sent him on his way.

He never filled his prescription.

ELEVEN

THE NEW HOUSE HAD SPARKED in us the feeling that we could fix all the things that were wrong with us. But I still wasn't doing so great with socializing. And the mental hospital had only *kind of* helped my dad. He had become Dad-Light — mostly jovial, but there was still something missing in him. He was never again quite as interested in the world around him, a little more interested in the papers he carried with him and the voices coming from the radio. He wasn't angry anymore, however, and I would take a jolly distracted dad over an angry distracted one any day. My mom was the only one of us left who had yet to fail at changing her life. I still believed that things would get better for us, and so when I was in fifth grade and she announced that she was going to have a series of spine surgeries to fix her back, I was optimistic that this was the change we'd all been waiting for.

The surgeries would, she said, keep her from shrinking even more than she already had. They would consist of steel rods being inserted into her back, which would gradually encourage her spine to straighten itself. Her doctor told her that she had the most severe case of scoliosis he had ever seen, and the surgeries would probably not correct her curvature completely, but they would help. She might one day have an almost normal body.

We spent an entire year preparing for these two magical surgeries. I spent my weekends in hospital waiting rooms waiting for my mother to come back with news from her surgeon or the results of X-rays and CT scans, or sitting at her side as she donated blood for the doctors to use during her surgery. Boring, but exciting. My mom was going to be normal.

In early July, a week before her first surgery, she told me that if anything were to go wrong during the surgery she had requested that she be allowed to die.

"I don't want to be a vegetable, and I couldn't live as a paraplegic," she said. "I want you to understand that if that happens, I wouldn't be happy."

I had always hoped that things were going to get better, but knew if there was an option to get worse, that that would probably happen. We weren't the kind of people that good things happened to.

She went on to tell me that she had designated a friend of hers to be her health care proxy, not wanting my father to have to make the choice to let her die.

"I don't want you to blame him," she said.

When I woke up on the day of her first surgery, she was already at the hospital. She and my father had gotten up early to check her in to pre-op, and I had stayed up late soaking in every last minute with my mom. We both cried as we said our good-byes the night before. We had convinced ourselves that this surgery was a bad idea, but there was no backing out now.

The first surgery consisted of her stomach being cut open

from navel to back, her organs removed so that her interverte-bral discs could be shaved and shaped to be make room for the rods.

I spent my day at summer camp, trying to succumb to the distraction of kickball and swimming lessons. When my father picked me up from camp, he said everything had gone accord-ing to plan, and I started to relax a bit. Things might be okay for us after all.

During the weeks of recovery between surgeries, my father would pick me up at my day camp after work and we would head to the hospital, where I would cuddle into Mom on her hospital bed and we would watch TV as a family. When visiting hours ended, my father and I would head to Wendy's, where he would get a cheeseburger and I would get a chili from the dollar menu.

I looked forward to these dollar menu dinners all day. My dad, without the distractions of the radio or his papers, was all mine for a moment in time, and I used it to my advantage, ask-ing him question after question about his life before me. He had told me there was a steel door in his head and that he couldn't access the memories behind it, and so stories of his youth were rare, but with enough prodding he revealed that he had been a track star in his teenage years. I learned he had a cousin who had made the Olympic team in track and field, and I learned that he had planned to follow in her footsteps until another kid on his team attacked him after practice one day.

"The kid was just messing around, he wasn't all right in the head," my father said. But the damage caused by the attack re-quired immediate surgery and put an end to my father's track career.

I learned about his time in the army. There was more than

one guy in his platoon named Jesus Christ, which he got a big kick out of. He spent a good portion of his time in basic training in the brig at Fort Gordon locked up for going AWOL. He didn't mean it, he said; he left because his mother was dying. He wanted to see her, and, not being one for protocol, he just picked up and headed back to New York. He came back to Georgia a few days later and was promptly arrested, but told me with a laugh, "These guys had mothers, too. I was locked up for awhile because that was what had to be done, but they counted the time as part of my service."

I found out that he was sent to Vietnam for a while after, but was eventually transferred to a base in Germany where he spent the remainder of his service.

"There was this one time," he said, already laughing, "this Hare Krishna started following me around, so I ducked into one of those blue-movie theaters to try and lose him, and he followed me right in. The two of us just stood there in the lobby of a porno theater together."

I was shocked that my father had actually tried to avoid the Hare Krishna. When missionaries came to our door with books about Latter-day Saints and Jehovah, my father would greet them all with a smile, take their books, and invite them to come back in a week or so to discuss the literature. When they would inevitably come back, my father would stand with them on the front lawn and discuss the reading. My mother wouldn't let me go out there with him, but I would quiz him about the religion of the week when he came back inside. Usually he'd ask if he could keep whatever book he'd borrowed, and he would pass off the books to me and encourage me to read them and see what I thought.

At home, after our Wendy's dinnertime interrogations were over, my dad would go to his room to look through his papers, and I would go to my mom's room and curl up to sleep with something from her closet that smelled like her.

By the time my mom's body had healed enough to partake in the second surgery, I had forgotten all about my paranoia. But when my father picked me up from camp the day of the second surgery, I could tell I had let down my guard a little too soon.

"Mom's surgery didn't work," he said as I buckled my seatbelt. Success and death were the only options I had considered; not working didn't seem like a possibility.

"Is she okay?"

"I don't know. We'll find out when we get to the hospital."

We listened to *All Things Considered* on the way to the hospital, and we didn't say anything else.

TWELVE

M Y MOM WAS STILL SLEEPING when we got to the hospital. Her doctor took my father aside to tell him about the surgery, and I stayed in the hospital room, staring at my mom. She was yellow and swollen. They'd cut her eyelashes off so that they could tape her eyes shut during surgery. She would hate that, I knew. My mother always told me how lucky I was to have black eyelashes. Hers were blond and took a great deal of mascara to become visible. I wouldn't need makeup like she did — she had ordered all my parts before I was born, she said. Her skin, Daddy's hair and straight back, Grandma's nose, and Grandpa's cleft chin. I turned out almost exactly as she'd planned, except for my legs — mine were not, even as a child, lean and shapely like hers, but instead thick and muscular like my father's.

"I forgot about the legs," she would say, apologizing. I would often brainstorm different traits I wanted my children to have one day. They all looked like some variation of me and Elijah Wood or Jonathan Brandis. I wouldn't forget minor details like legs.

She hadn't looked as bad after the previous surgery. Now,

even in her sleep, she looked defeated, a look she would never quite shake. Her body was huge — she had almost doubled in size from the bloat and bandages. This surgery had opened her from the nape of her neck to the bottom of her tailbone, and the doctors had closed her skin with giant staples that stuck out from her hospital gown.

I went outside to cry. I didn't want her to wake up and see how scared I was, scared that my mother would be permanently damaged. Scared that I would have to rely on my father to take care of me, and scared to admit that I didn't really trust him to do it.

I had cried myself out by the time my dad had gotten back and had started to doze off, a combination of spending all day in the sun and being emotionally exhausted.

As he nudged me awake, I questioned him: "What did the doctor say?"

"He said that Mom's vertebrae were fused together, so they couldn't put the rods in." We stared at each other for a few minutes, neither of us knowing what to do next.

All the tests my mom had taken hadn't revealed to the doctors that her spine had started to fuse to itself where her curvature was most acute. Putting the rods in would have pulled her vertebrae apart, potentially paralyzing her.

"Come on," he said. "The anesthesia should wear off soon. Let's go wait for Mom to wake up."

There was nothing else to be done. My mother would be sent home in a few days to heal. Her abdominal muscles had been cut open during the first surgery and she could no longer walk on her own — she would spend the summer in bed, and then the fall, winter, and following spring. Her body was fitted for a plastic brace that would be used in the few instances she needed to be wheeled outside of the house. The brace would do the heavy lifting of keeping her upright until her own body was once again capable.

The government job she'd had for years didn't wait for her to recover; she lost her job while her body struggled to once again become functional. She had been the breadwinner of our family. She might not have been able to keep a clean house, but my mom could take care of us — and now she couldn't even sit up without help.

Stranded in bed, she far preferred the company of the television to me. I didn't understand her depression; I just knew that my mom, my one stabilizing force, wanted nothing to do with life.

THIRTEEN

FTER HER SURGERY all my mother wanted to eat was fruit, so my father would cut up slices of watermelon and cantaloupe to leave by her bed for her to eat throughout the day while he went to work. He had started working again as a school bus driver. He made far less driving school buses than he had working for the MTA, but the hours meant he could come home during his lunch break and check on my mother, make sure she was still stocked on melon and rub cocoa butter into her scars, and still be home early enough to drive me to dance class after school.

Without my mother to cook for us, my father and I subsisted mainly on fast food and microwaved hot dogs.

My father seemed to function better when he worked — having a place to go during the day and a paycheck to show for it seemed to keep him engaged in the world a bit more. Engaged, but still messy. With my mother bedridden, there was no one to keep him in check, no constant nagging to keep his papers off the kitchen table, dining room table, and couches. The house filled with flyers, books, and newspapers. He expanded his horizons to anything he could find in the clearance aisles of Kmart or Caldor, mostly gadgets missing parts, books with missing covers, and tools that had been separated from the rest of their set. My mother started joining in. After I would leave for school and my father for work, she was alone all day with nothing but television to keep her company. She spent her days ordering things from Home Shopping Network and QVC.

Each day, I would come home from school to piles of UPS boxes waiting outside our door. By now, the house had already started to look unkempt, the grass overgrown and the paint chipping. If he could see inside our drapes, the UPS man would have seen mountains of the boxes he delivered each day, many never opened, surrounded by walls of paper and garbage bags. I wondered what he thought of us, if he ever skipped knocking and just ditched the packages outside. But then again, I wondered what everyone thought of us.

I hated my mother for being in a wheelchair. When she was in bed, I could tell myself that she was relaxing, letting her body heal. But once a week, she would pull herself into a sitting position, and my father would help her into the big plastic brace she wore from her tailbone to her chest. While he did that, I was responsible for cleaning from off the stairs whatever debris had collected there so that she wouldn't slip on anything on the way down.

She just wanted to be out of the house, she said; she didn't care where we went. And so we usually ended up at grocery or department stores. Shopping always seemed like the only thing there ever was to do. My father pushed her down the aisles, and I would get lost among the shelves, doing everything in my power not to be seen with her. People stare at people in wheelchairs, and I had made it a practice to be noticed as little as possible.

In my memory, the years that come after my mother's surgeries are a haze, and I suppose that is what we were living in.

By the time sixth grade started, I had stopped speaking aloud almost entirely, and the school wrote home to inform my parents that another girl had been assigned the duty of speaking for me because I refused.

My mother signed me up for acting classes advertised in the local Pennysaver, desperate for any activity that might force me to interact with other children at an audible level. She was vacillating between the mom I had always known, nurturing and protective, and being completely apathetic. She was at her best in the morning before she had a chance to spend the day wallowing. In the mornings, she would sip coffee while I ate breakfast, and we would talk like we always had. But inevitably the conversation would turn to her deformities, exacerbated by the surgeries, the constant pain she was feeling and the worthless creature she said she had become. By the time I got home from school, she was gone for the day, lost in her own world.

FOURTEEN

Y PARENTS PROMISED to wait in the parking lot in case I needed to make a quick getaway, but when my first three-hour basic acting class was finished, I took my spot in the backseat and said, "I like it."

It took a couple of hours to get to that point, though. When I first walked into the musty old barn theater, I took a seat in the last row while all the other kids in class promptly filled out the first two rows. The teacher, with her long curly black hair and breasts that seemed to take up the entirety of her abdomen, stood on stage introducing us to the theater. Stages were once built on a slant, she told us, so *upstage* meant toward the back, *downstage* toward the front. I soaked in the vocabulary, repeating stage directions — *up, down, stage right, stage left* — over and over again in my head so I wouldn't embarrass myself when the time came to stand in front of everyone.

My hiding spot was outed by the attendance sheet, and I was forced to join the rest of the class in the front of the theater, where I was subject to all the same vocal warm-ups, improv games, and scene readings that the other kids were. When the teacher walked around handing out scenes, she looked at each of us, evaluating what she saw during our warm-up games, and handed me the part of Fern from *A Rosen by Any Other Name.* Sweet and moderately boring, the prepubescent love scene took place via a phone call, so I wouldn't actually have to interact physically with my scene partner. I wouldn't have, anyway — I barely interacted with the hand I used as my prop phone, instead focusing all of my energy on the three stapled pages of photocopied budding romance. I didn't dare look up when my acting teacher yelled at me to speak louder.

The voice I conjured in my head sounded like she was screaming, but the actual voice that came out was only slightly louder than a whisper. Even so, I felt comfortable onstage with Fern's words to keep me company. I didn't have to think of anything to say, I didn't have to worry about embarrassing myself, and I didn't have to worry about anyone asking any questions about me. All anyone wanted to know about was Fern.

Speaking above a whisper still felt like an overwhelmingly revealing task in school, and the girl who sat next to me in class still had to answer my teacher's questions for me, but onstage, I felt safe behind the guard of whoever I was playing. In acting class, I was encouraged to talk about my character in the first person, and I knew that the audience would judge my character's personalities and feelings — not mine. So I savored every single raw emotion my acting teacher instructed me to feel. The characters I played were people that existed solely on paper, yet their words and feelings were so much more tangible to me than my own. I started to convince myself that I might just be able to create a character to use in real life as my own personal security blanket.

The opportunity to test out this strategy was provided by my seventh grade English teacher — a skinny man with a round head and neatly trimmed white beard. Mr. Griffith noticed me, quiet and invisible as I tried to be. He had a crisp, quiet voice, but he used it to command attention. Mr. Griffith seemed to truly respect the literary insights of his twelve-year-old students, but had no tolerance for the boys in my class who answered his questions about symbolism and Steinbeck in mocking effeminate tones. I liked him immediately, but he never let on that he felt the same about me. Instead, he called my mother shortly after the school year started to inform her that he had already spoken with the rest of my seventh grade teachers and, with my parents' approval, wanted to change my curriculum to put me in class with the advanced students.

I had never considered myself particularly smart. My father was brilliant, but I didn't want to be like him, as I was convinced it was his brilliance that made him strange. What I did want was a fresh start and a chance to be someone else. I would settle for smart, if it came with a clean slate.

The "smart kids" were a cloistered group unto themselves. I didn't know them, and more important, they didn't know me. What I saw was a group of well-rounded, micromanaged prodigies who were exceptional in all arenas of middle school life. I decided I would use this as a template to create a new Kim.

Just like the monologues and scenes I spent my weekends rehearsing for acting class, the character I was creating required practice and research. I created role models out of other kids in my class, watching what they did and mimicking vocabulary, mannerisms, and favored topics of discussion. I cut pictures of models and actresses out of magazines and glued them to the inside of my notebooks, perfect people to channel when I was sure that my own personality was lacking. I gave myself period-long pep talks before lunch to muster the courage to ask to sit with new people and try out these well-practiced topics of conversation. I created a set of "normal kid" problems to fall back on when a conversation with my new social circle was complaint-based, pretending that my parents were sticklers for grades and appearance. I was too old for make-believe, so I simply tried on one lie after another until I created the person I wanted to be.

Anna was the first person in my new social circle with whom I became close. We sat next to one another in French; I was good at French, but she was better, understanding the nuances of the language in a matter of months. When the teacher realized her aptitude, she was allowed to take more and more language courses, first adding Spanish and then Italian to her course load. Tenses and vocabulary lessons gave us something to talk about, but it was obvious from early on that Anna was one of those people that just liked everyone, and in return, it would be hard to find someone in our grade, regardless of social hierarchy, who didn't like her. It helped that she lived a few blocks from me and was an easy walk from my house.

Anna's parents were both teachers, and her house reflected that love of learning. Mind-teasing games could be found on every surface, and the walls of her living room were lined with books. Her parents loved information just as much as my dad did, and there were books and newspapers and knickknacks in Anna's house, too, but they never took over. On the days my dad would drive over to pick me up, I wanted nothing more than to invite him into my new friend's house and show him what our home could look like.

I also envied her family's heritage — they were 100-percent Italian, unlike my family that was full of mixed-breeds. Everything about Anna's family was identifiable as Italian, from the tiles on her kitchen floor to the food they cooked to the way Anna looked, with her heart-shaped face, big brown doelike eyes, thick brown hair, and womanly-even-in-seventh-grade figure. Anna had come into this world with an identity already waiting for her.

I was amazed by her ability to react to things, to laugh fully when things were funny, to cry when they were sad, and to turn a bright red when they were embarrassing. Anna seemed to feel everything deeply, while I was constantly trying not to feel anything at all.

I slept over Anna's house often, and when her parents would go to sleep, we would inevitably find ourselves in the kitchen making pasta or pancakes; afterward, we would sit on the floor to eat them, always at my request. Sitting on the floor was no longer an option at my house.

"You know," she said, head in the refrigerator, searching for syrup, "you never *don't* look happy."

"What do you mean?"

"I mean you can't say anything without smiling. Even when you're saying things that don't go with a smile."

I took her psychoanalysis as a compliment: I was pulling off happy.

. . .

Anna introduced me to her group of friends, who accepted me easily. They had adopted another new member to their gaggle recently, a girl named Rachel who had just transferred from another middle school.

Rachel looked like the kind of twelve-year-old you knew would grow up to be beautiful: slightly built, with brown hair down to her waist, perfectly straight bangs, and legs that reached the ceiling. She was new to our school and already the topic of curious whispers between classes — a popular girl in the making. Rachel looked familiar to me, and at lunch, we pieced together that we had been running into each other for awhile. We had both been in the NICU at the same hospital at the same time as babies. She was five months older than I was, but had meningitis as an infant. We had taken the same dance class years earlier and also worked on an article together in the newspaper club in the children's section of the local library.

My father loved the library and was constantly paying fines for the books he took out and never returned because they had been lost somewhere in the house. When we first moved to the area after our house burned down, he had spent a good amount of time getting to know the library stacks and staff. He'd heard about the library club from the children's librarian and immediately signed me up. He was so excited about the idea of me writing for a newspaper that I didn't tell him I couldn't think of anything I'd like to do less. He hadn't been excited about anything for a long time.

My first ever article was about prejudice, and Rachel had been my partner. After school that day when we made the connection, I brought up the newspaper club to my dad, and he fished through one of his dresser drawers to pull out the small yellowed newspaper with a cover article about prejudice and tolerance that I had written years earlier — Rachel and I shared the byline.

Through Anna and Rachel, I met more and more people and made more and more friends. I still wasn't an extrovert by any means, but I was acting like I had a modicum of social grace.

FIFTEEN

I T WOULD BE YEARS before I heard the theory that hoarders tend to be perfectionists, that each item they collect is one crucial part of an ideal world they are ever creating for themselves. If that's the case, it's possible I inherited this, too, from my father. The older I got, the more obsessed I became with maintaining the illusion that everything in my life was perfect — and as the years passed, I depended upon it to fly me under the radar of friends and faculty long enough to get to college.

No one questions the home life of quiet girls with good grades and kickline practice after school. My need to be seen as perfect was as compulsive as my father's need to surround himself with paper.

By the time I got to high school, my act had become second nature. I wasn't the shy, barely audible girl I'd been when I was younger. I had people to wave to in the hallways and to pass notes to in class, and parties to go to on the weekend. I was nicknamed "Kimbie" by my new social circle and took on a persona to match my peppy nickname. I rarely left school before 7 p.m. because I had become so immersed in the social world of extracurricular activities, each one chosen as a notch for my college applications and intended to illustrate just how well-rounded I was.

I didn't rebel like other kids my age did. I didn't long to be kissed by boys or wear brand-name jeans. My wildest fantasy — the focus of all my efforts — was college. College would rescue me. On paper, I was the all-American girl. At home, things had reached an unfathomable level of squalor.

Between my father's love of paper (and just about everything else he could get his hands on) and my mother's depression-fueled shopping, our house had started to resemble the remnants at the bottom of a garbage can. Soggy junk filled our living space. When I was fourteen, the boiler broke in the middle of winter, but we could never allow a repairman into our mess, and so we lived without heat, without showers. Instead we joined a local gym (I lied and said I was sixteen), and each Sunday we would go through the motions of a workout so that we would feel justified in using the locker room for our weekly shower.

I was lucky: Instead of acne, puberty had brought with it dry skin and dry hair. I could go a week without washing my hair and still look presentable. Rubbing alcohol and cotton balls sufficed for spot hygiene maintenance to keep body odor under control.

Later — I don't remember precisely when — the pipes in our house started to decay, causing flooding throughout the house. We shut the water off at regular intervals, turning it on to flush the toilet a few times a day, knowing that each time we allowed the water to flow, moisture would escape and drip through the downstairs ceiling that had started to rot. The house smelled musty and moldy, and my trips to the ER for asthma attacks had become so frequent that the hospital eventually sent me home with a nebulizer of my own. Two out of our three bathrooms had stopped working because of various levels of disrepair, so we all used one bathroom on the second floor. The door no longer closed all the way because there was too much junk in the hallway, and no matter how many times we pushed it away, the junk would eventually fall back into its rightful place. We settled for pushing the door closed as far as we could for maximum privacy. Unused, the tub had been converted to yet another place to hold things.

Fleas were as much a part of our summers as swimming and ice cream. The dogs would bring them in from the backyard, but we couldn't set off a bug bomb and get rid of them like our neighbors did — there were too many places amid the trash for them to hide. We spent the summers being eaten alive by them. I would capture them between my thumb and forefinger and cut their slim little bodies in half with my fingernail, watching my own blood seep from their severed bodies.

I could pass the fleabites off as mosquito bites most of the time, but there was a constant fear that one would jump from my hair or clothes in school and people would see them. That people would know that I was flea-infested.

The dogs fared worse than we did, though; there weren't enough flea collars in the world to keep them safe. I hated seeing my little cocker spaniel Jewel's coat turn from light blond to a rusty red color from the fleas' blood-drenched dander.

The downstairs had become a relative swamp ground. It never seemed to dry out from the flooding, so when we did walk through it, the inches of trash would squish beneath our feet, creating an unsteady terrain. The living room, dining room, and den — spaces I thought my father would never find enough things to fill — had floor-to-ceiling piles of boxes and bags of paper and knickknacks, things that had been purchased and put down and long forgotten. We gave up the kitchen and survived solely on fast food and hermetically sealed snacks we could keep in our bedrooms.

I often felt like I had two different families. There was the family we were at home, where we lived every man for himself. There wasn't room anywhere anymore, in the four-bedroom house with the two-car garage and attic big enough to convert to an apartment, for us all to fit somewhere together, so we each found our own station. My mother spent most of her time on the small corner of mattress that was left for her to sleep. Over the years, her mattress had started to slide off the box spring, pushed aside by the spoils of her constant shopping. The side of the bed she slept on teetered at a 45-degree angle, while the half of her mattress still firmly planted on a flat surface had been taken over by stuff. The rest of her time was spent in front of the computer. As the house deteriorated, so had my parents' friendships, and so my mother spent most of her time talking with people she had met in AOL chat rooms, people who couldn't see her twisted body or garbage-filled house.

My father either sat on his mattress in the sea of paper that was his bedroom or in the driver's side of the car, and I had my room.

My bedroom was no better than the rest of the house. My parents, especially my mother, were generous in their shopping. Lacking for anything was never my problem, but I didn't value anything I owned. Everything that came into my house was garbage. It was easier to throw out my dirty clothes than to get the width of a laundry basket through the front door to a Laundromat. Every few months I would purge my room of the dirty clothes, unused spoils of late night shopping binges, and hallway debris that made its way into my haven into big black plastic bags until the floor was visible, but it would only be a matter of weeks before I had new things and new clothes to take their place.

The family we were outside the house was completely different. My father arranged his work schedule around shuttling me to my seemingly endless array of afterschool activities. I would go to kickline, voice lessons, and youth ambulance corp meetings, while he and my mother would wait in the car. Over the years, they'd gone from fighting all the time to barely talking at all while in the confines of the house, but in the car they were still the same. When I would come out from dance class or acting class or my voice lessons or from a brunch shift at the restaurant I waitressed at, they were there, laughing.

"Hi, honey, how was class?" was my mother's standard greeting, followed by "Okay, kiddo, where to next?" from my dad. And there always was a next place to be. We ate out almost every night, a byproduct of having abandoned the kitchen. In these moments, at restaurants, we were at our best, because unlike in the car, which was almost always filled with bags of my father's papers, in a restaurant we were completely free. We laughed — loud, and often at the kind of humor that only seems to make sense in families. My father could laugh so loud and for so long that the people seated around us would start laughing, too.

Life lessons were dished out over appetizers. Over a basket

of buffalo wings, my parents set the ground rules for drugs and alcohol.

"I don't need to know what you do; I just want you to call me to pick you up after you've done it," my father said.

"What if it's late?"

"I don't care how late it is," he said. "I just don't want you getting into a car with someone who's been drinking."

"I'd rather you didn't drink, either. It's in your blood, honey. Your grandparents were alcoholics," my mother chimed in. "If you have to choose, I'd rather you smoked pot — it's not addictive."

"If alcoholism bypassed Dad, I think it will bypass me."

"When I first met your father, he drank quite heavily," she told me, looking over at my father. "I told him if he wanted to keep seeing me, he'd have to give up drinking, and he did."

My dad went to go "vote," which was his euphemism for using the bathroom, and I started in on my mom. I was always trying to get to the bottom of who my dad was before I knew him.

"You've seen dad drunk?"

"Oh yeah, he was quite amorous. There wasn't a girl in a bar that was safe once your father had a few beers in him."

I could picture him as a silly drunk, but affectionate seemed wholly out of character. I could count on one hand the number of times my parents had kissed on the lips.

When my father came back to the table, we caught him up on our conversation, and his grin broadened as he told the story of the night my parents met — at an orgy, in 1973.

My father loved telling this story. I couldn't remember the first time I had heard it, but I remembered being immediately embarrassed by it. My parents couldn't even meet like normal parents. After sharing it with Rachel and Anna to shocked giggles, I started milking it for all the entertainment value it was worth at parties and sleepovers. But the truth was — as far as orgies go — this one was relatively G-rated, at least for my parents.

My parents referred to it as "the party," because my mother apparently didn't notice the part of the invitation that mentioned that group sex would be on the itinerary and showed up thinking she was going to a run-of-the-mill house party.

My father, newly back from the army, knew exactly what he was getting into, and unfortunately for him, this was the one and only orgy he had ever been invited to — unfortunate because the little redhead he was flirting with when the party transitioned from chitchat in the living room to naked bonding in the bedroom grabbed ahold of his arm and asked him if he would mind staying with her in the living room, just to talk.

"I couldn't leave her there. Plus, that finger thing she was doing was nice, running her index finger up and down my forearm . . ." my father said.

My mom just giggled nervously. "I thought it was a party!"

My parents spent the evening flirting in the living room while their friends got it on in the bedroom.

When I've told that story to friends over the years, I'm often asked if I was conceived that night — I wasn't. My parents didn't become a couple right away. What started that night was an indelible friendship. My parents didn't curl up at night and talk about feelings, but they enrolled in college together, spending their downtime at movies or hustling pool at local bars.

It was while playing pool one night, about a year into their friendship, that they made the transition from friends to something more.

"The guy I was playing opposite was being very attentive," my mother says. "All of a sudden, your father was all over me, in a way he'd never been before. So that was that."

Shortly afterward, they moved in together, and a few years after that, they decided to leave the cramped spaces and paper-thin walls of apartment living behind them and move to a house on Long Island. Two years after that, they decided to have a child. Two years after *that*, my mother found out she was pregnant, and finally, on the seventh anniversary of their pool-table kindling, they got married.

My parents used to have adventures — leave for a drive around the neighborhood only to embark on a days-long road trip, or dress in drag for a night out — just to make each other laugh.

I could sit in restaurants or parking lots with my parents forever, because I knew as soon as we pulled into our driveway, my family would disband and we'd all go back into hiding.

SIXTEEN

AN INSTRUMENTAL PART OF MY façade was my decoy house. The more friends I made, the more likely it was that their parents would offer me a ride home. But I was too embarrassed to let anyone see me walk into my own house. The garage door no longer shut completely — something had been long broken in the mechanism that allowed it to lock, and so every so often it would inch up to reveal the massive piles of long-forgotten treasures that had taken over the garage. The panels opposite the front door were rotting, the wood gradually chipping away, with a plastic bag taped to the outside as its only source of insulation. My biggest fear would be that a friend would be in the neighborhood and want to drop by, knocking on the door, only to see the spiderwebs and dead moths and flies that made their home in our curtains, or see through our window shades to the teetering piles behind them.

The house I chose was completely unremarkable. Small and neatly kept, it was the kind of house you forgot was there, and it was exactly what I wished I had. My decoy was five houses away, around the corner from my real house. It was easy for people to drop me off and continue on down the road. Not too far a walk from my real house, but far enough to ensure that they'd be back on the road by the time I arrived at my door. I didn't know the people who lived there, and if someone were ever to knock on their door looking for me, I would have to come up with some sort of excuse, but at least my secret would still be safe.

Mr. Griffith died in a car accident during my junior year of high school. I hadn't seen him since seventh grade English class. I was a totally different girl because of him. His death devastated me as it was relayed as gossip between classes. When I told my mother, we both cried. "That man changed your life," she said.

I didn't want to seem overly dramatic, so I kept my mourning to myself during school hours, but at home I cried for weeks over my fallen hero. I wondered how many other kids would go unchampioned now that he was gone.

SEVENTEEN

WHILE DOING HOMEWORK in my room my senior year of high school, I saw a report on the evening news about a local family "living in filth." My heart stopped when the reporter standing outside the worn brown ranch house commented on the "disgusting" living conditions inside. It wasn't *my* house the perfectly coifed reporter was standing in front of, but it may as well have been. I scanned the image onscreen and saw so many similarities in the deteriorating building: random pieces of furniture sitting on the side of the house along with the trash, shrubbery allowed to run wild to shield the prying eyes of passersby, curtains drawn in every window. I wanted to know everything about that house — where it was, who lived in it, if there were kids there. And I wanted throw up, because it wasn't my house but it was my secret, and it was out there in the open.

The reporter said that the owner suffered from a rare obsessive-compulsive disorder called "hoarding." Before the report was over, I was running into my mother's room.

"Turn on channel four!" I yelled as I burst through the door, but the segment had already ended.

"There are other people who live like us! It was on the news."

"No one lives like us, Kim. No one else would ever live like this."

"They do! There's a condition called *hoarding*. I think that's what Dad has."

"Your father doesn't have anything other than a severe case of not caring about anyone but himself and his papers."

I didn't let my mother's disbelief dampen my bitter excitement. There was now a word for my father, and having a word meant that we weren't alone in this.

Boston, Europe, Los Angeles

EIGHTEEN

I PURPOSEFULLY REDIRECTED MY route between
classes to take me past the guidance office. In the front window, there were paper stars with the names of graduating
seniors and the colleges they'd been accepted to.

"Another one?" the secretary asked as I handed her my latest
acceptance letter, my twelfth. I'd been a bit overzealous during
application season, getting lost in the fantasy world of college
brochures: pictures of young men and women, a little older than
I was, smiling while on line in pristine dining halls or in neatly
decorated dorm rooms, and pictures of well-dressed professors
in front of projector screens. Each school had its own personality and potential for a new life.

Of my twelve schools, there were two I was seriously debat-
ing between. Syracuse University had offered me a full scholarship, and it was certainly my parents' pick for me. My father
started wearing an Orangemen baseball cap with his uniform to
work each morning, and my mother touted the importance of
starting my adult life debt-free. I wasn't quite as sure. I had visited Syracuse in January when there was two feet of snow on the
ground. My nose hairs froze on the walk from the hotel to the

acting school auditions, and my long-deliberated, perfect college audition outfit was drenched up to my midthighs thanks to the unshoveled sidewalks.

Syracuse was practical, but my dream school was in Boston.

One year earlier, I hadn't even heard of Emerson College, but a school trip to Boston my junior year had changed all that. In an offhand comment, our tour guide had introduced the small liberal arts school as Boston's playground for artistic freaks and geeks. While on the outside, I may have strongly resembled a Gap ad, on the inside I was all freak. It didn't hurt that it was a balmy spring day and the Boston Commons were in full bloom. Our tour guide didn't mention that Boston could be every bit the arctic tundra that upstate New York was during the winter.

Unlike my runner-up, Emerson was known for being incredibly stingy when it came to financial aid, and in my searches I found it on "worst of" lists when it came to financial services.

When my aid packages started rolling in from the schools around the Northeast, it became clear that Emerson could take or leave me. The tiny school in Boston gave me a small amount of need-based aid and nothing for my academic achievements and pages of carefully planned extracurricular activities.

Still, Emerson was the biggest crush I'd ever had, and I was determined to make it work for me. I couldn't picture myself anywhere else. I started crunching numbers: After my scholarship, I would need $19,000 a year just for tuition, plus money for room, board, and expenses. If I worked full-time in addition to my school load, I might be able to cover it.

I quit the kickline in December of my senior year so that I could pick up more waitressing shifts, and I spent my downtime scoping out restaurants in Boston travel guides and calling to see if they'd be hiring come September. I took out books about scholarships and financial aid from the library and put calls in to the financial aid department to ask if I qualified for work-study. If I worked the maximum allotment of student labor hours, I could take another $2,000 off my bill.

While my parents favored Syracuse for their own reasons, they told me that it was ultimately my choice. They weren't paying for college, so it was my decision and mine alone. And so on Labor Day weekend of 2000, in typical Miller fashion, my parents and I loaded up a U-Haul with more stuff than I could possibly ever need and hit the I-90.

Unlike the sprawling quads my friends were moving to, Emerson's campus was the Boston Commons. My dorm was beautiful, an office building converted into student apartments. From my window, I could watch Boston's businesspeople rushing to meetings, students rushing to class, derelicts napping in the sun, and the weathered tombstones of Revolutionary War–era icons holding their historical ground in the cemetery amidst the park. Most important, it was new and it was clean. My college home was picture perfect, as were my roommates. My freshman suite came complete with three bedrooms and three roommates, all of whom were smart, friendly, strikingly attractive — and who, strangely enough, seemed to like me. It was like I'd finally managed to be the girl I'd been pretending to be for so long. Once we'd finished lugging my suitcases and Yaffa blocks upstairs, I immediately kicked my parents out.

"I'm going down to the dining hall with my roommates," I said, a not-too-subtle hint that my parents should make their way back to Long Island. While this should have been a milestone moment for us as a family, I really just wanted them to leave before anyone started to see the cracks in my façade.

"Don't you want to go out to eat? Say good-bye?" my mom asked me, while smiling at the snub. Years before, she had put me in acting lessons — not to fuel my creative fire but to get me to speak to other kids. Now I was majoring in acting and talking to people all by myself.

As a little girl, I used to lie in bed, thinking *Maybe if I endure all my pain now, I could be happy when I am older.* Emerson felt like my reward for the years of shame I'd logged. No one there knew about the hate-fueled letters our neighbors left in our mailbox. They didn't know how much I appreciated cafeteria food after having spent most of my teenage years eating hermetically sealed, chemically laden foods, because our kitchen had been left to rot under cobwebs and maggots. I no longer had to plan meetings with friends so they wouldn't know where I lived. There would be no more walks down the block to stand in front of a stranger's home when someone announced they were on their way. I loved being able to shower without fear that rotten pipes would create a flood. For the first time in my life, I felt normal.

My freshman year was like a movie montage. I'd never been so happy. I spent my days learning with people who were creative and talented and who thought that I was, too. When I wasn't working, my nights were spent hopping from dorm room to dorm room visiting friends and doing *Abs of Steel* videos with my roommates, followed by trips to the c-store for some Ben & Jerry's, or playing tourist in my beautiful new hometown.

My roommates and I made plans to study abroad together in the Netherlands our sophomore year and set about comparing backpacks and making lists of the countries we'd visit together on weekends. But as May approached, the reality that the school year was coming to a close started to set in. While my new friends and I made promises to visit one another in the coming months, I found myself preparing lies about family vacations and remodeling work — lies to break out if any of these plans came to fruition. The old Kim enveloped me like a dank, moth-holed blanket just waiting to welcome me home.

When I returned to New York, the things that had been so normal to me before — the rats, the sludge, the ubiquitous smell of mildew, the feeling that this was my home — were glaringly wrong. I couldn't get used to them again.

And I could hardly speak to the parents I had once been so afraid of hurting. At school, I could pretend that I was like everyone else, but I couldn't pretend at home. At home, I was dirty. I spent my summer doing what I had always done: being too busy to be home. I worked days as a waitress and nights as a security guard. I slept at Rachel's house during my free nights; she even had an extra mattress on her floor that was designated for me. But I couldn't sleep there forever — my seemingly endless presence had already been the source of fighting between Rachel and her sister.

One night, after a waitressing shift of her own, Rachel's sister came into Rachel's room asking to sleep on the mattress on the floor.

"Doesn't she have her own home?" she asked Rachel, not looking at me.

When she left, I asked why Rachel's sister wanted to sleep in her room. "She started redecorating her room this morning and it's a mess, so she wants to sleep here," Rachel said.

I was already self-conscious about the amount of time I spent at my friend's house, but now I was completely mortified. I made a mental note to avoid Rachel. It was time to go back home.

At home, the nights were sleepless. It was the rats. In high school when the rats had kept me up, my mother and I would get in the car and drive to a twenty-four-hour grocery store, but my mother had started working again when I went to college, taking an overnight job as a security dispatcher. With no one with whom to escape, I would try to suck up my fear alone, but as soon as I started to doze off, I'd hear a squeak or the shuffle of papers, and I would know the rats were in my room. One even made it up to my bed once, scurrying across my leg like a hurdler. After that, I started sleeping in my car. I would take my blanket and pillow and curl up in the backseat of my 1988 Pontiac Grand Am. All I wanted was for school to start again.

In mid-July, a letter came from the Emerson financial aid department. I had a small trust in my name from an accident I'd had as a child that was set up so that I wouldn't be able to access the funds until I was twenty-one. But because that trust existed, the school decided that I no longer qualified for financial aid.

Without financial aid, I couldn't go back to Emerson. I couldn't take out the kinds of loans necessary to pay for the pricey private school. I was majoring in theater, and even at eighteen, I knew that I would never be able to pay back that kind of debt on a waitress's salary. I called the school and tried to explain, but the financial aid officer professed that until those funds were utilized they wouldn't be required to give me any need-based aid. But I wouldn't be able to touch that money until halfway through my senior year of college.

The room started spinning. There was only a month left of summer, and I was already working full-time in addition to school. I started to break down on the phone, and the man on the other end of the line became annoyed. I had never been very good at fighting my own battles. As she had done so many times before, my mother took over. She tried to explain that she and my father weren't financially able to help me with tuition, that she had been disabled for years, and that my father drove a school bus. "She's already working two jobs to pay for school," she pleaded. Then she started yelling. Eventually she hung up.

"What did he say?"

"You don't want to go there, anyway." She responded in an indignant huff, but we both knew that it wasn't true. All I wanted was to go back to Emerson.

I waited a moment, then ventured the question again. "What did he say?"

"He said that if you can't afford it, then you don't belong there." She was livid that anyone could say something like that, but I wasn't.

It was true. My freshman year I was assigned to a group project with a girl whose father was a famous musician, a guy whose family owned the largest chain of electronics stores in the Northeast, and another guy whose father ran a record label. I didn't belong at Emerson with all the perfect, beautiful kids with their trust funds and summer homes. I belonged here, among the sludge and rot.

I didn't know what I was going to do. It was too late in the summer to apply to be a transfer student at a good school, and there was no way I'd be able to get housing anywhere at this point. I had to move back home.

I spent the next week pretending that nothing in my life had changed, putting off making a decision about my future, and hoping that some rich Hamptonian would roll into my small town and leave me a $40,000 tip. After an overnight of security-guard duty and a morning of serving brunch, I came home that Saturday to find my parents on the front lawn, arms flailing and voices raised, having an argument with our neighbors. The neighbors and their three young children stood on their side of the lawn, the markedly greener and more evenly cut side. What I could garner from the back-and-forth was that our rottweiler, Gretchen, had gotten loose, dug into their backyard, and barked at their daughters. They had called animal control. They wanted her put down.

One of the best parts of my childhood had been that my mother was a dog breeder. I didn't have siblings, but I always had puppies around to play with. The dogs weren't always kept in the best of conditions, but despite their matted coats and cramped cage-living arrangement, they loved us unconditionally, and they made me feel safe in an environment that often felt scary.

In addition to two cocker spaniels, we had Gretchen. My big, sweet Gretchen looked vicious, but she didn't know that. She thought she was a lap dog and would often curl all 110 pounds of herself onto the nearest warm body and wait for her ears to be scratched. When pint-sized Jewel snarled and snapped to show her dominance as the alpha of the clan, Gretchen would simply pin her down with her paws and wag her tongue and tail. It was a game to her, and she'd never so much as nipped anything that wasn't kibble. But, because our neighbors were scared of us, they were scared of her. To them, she was just a junkyard dog guarding the house of garbage.

Shortly after I arrived, the conversation broke up, each party returning to their own house to badmouth each other.

"We're going to bring Gretchen to the pound," my mother announced with dejected resolve.

"How can you just let them do this? She didn't bite anyone!"

"I can't, Kim. If I fought them, they'd come to the house. Why don't you get a little rest? You must be tired." There was no fight left in her as she leashed Gretchen and took her out to the car.

I thought that I should cry, that's what a normal person would do, but the tears didn't come. I was empty.

I had never thought about killing myself before. I'd always had something to live for — the future. Whenever things seemed like they were too much, I thought about how amazing my life would be one day when I was an actress. When I was onstage, playing someone else, I could experience all kinds of emotions — emotions I had spent years compartmentalizing so that they wouldn't hurt anyone else's feelings. I couldn't tell my dad how ashamed he made me without hurting him, and I knew that if I cried to my mother she'd feel like a failure. Onstage, I could yell. I could scream and cry — I could let it all out, all under the guise of a character. But I wasn't going to be an actress anymore. I couldn't come up with the kind of money I needed to go back to Emerson in four weeks. I was stuck here, where the world was joyless and broken, where I couldn't even have a dog to protect me from the rats.

I didn't think "I'm going to kill myself now" when I walked to the bathroom, but once I was there, the medicine cabinet called out to me. I grabbed a bottle of painkillers off the shelf. I felt like there was no way to leave this house — it would always drag me back. I had tried to escape, and I had failed.

I carried the bottle back to my bedroom and poured the painkillers onto the sheetless twin bed. A fistful consisted of nineteen pills; they looked so small. I used a warm bottle of Diet Pepsi that had been sitting next to my bed to swallow them in three-to-four-pill increments. Pills that small couldn't possibly kill me. I took a few more. I left six pills in the jar in case my parents needed them later.

I lay down and traced the outline of the mattress's design with my finger until the tears finally came.

I was scared it might be painful. I was worried about my parents. I wondered if my mom would kill herself, too. It seemed like something she might do. But then my dad would be alone. Who would take care of him?

I thought about my parents finding my body. I imagined them dragging it down the stairs and maneuvering it through the front door.

Even if we wanted to open the door and let the whole world in, we couldn't. The piles of old clothes, shoes, papers long-rotted and mâché'd from flooding, an old plastic Christmas tree still decorated from a long-past holiday, and a still new-in-the-box air-conditioner in the foyer made it impossible to open the door more than ten inches — and even that took a good deal of force.

And so, I thought of my parents steering my body sideways, as we had to do to get in and out, to bring me out to the front yard, where an ambulance, or maybe a hearse, could come gather me up.

I could go throw up now, I thought. *It could still be okay.*

I didn't throw up. I didn't want my life anymore.

Somewhere along the way, I realized that I'd stopped crying and that the world was moving a little slower. I wasn't thinking about my parents anymore, but instead focusing on the swooshing sound of the blood throbbing in my ears. It was calming, repetitive.

And then my parents came home from bringing Gretchen to the pound. Maybe I'd been right about the pills being too small, or maybe it just took more time to die. My mom came into my room to check on me and knew immediately what had happened in her absence. She's always been like that.

"Kim, what did you do? What did you take?" She was yelling at me.

Then she started screaming for my dad, who said nothing, but robotically threw me over his shoulder, fireman-style, the way he had so many times when I was a little girl, and carried me out to the car.

Ten minutes later I was in the ER with a charcoal smoothie to suck on.

Overdosing didn't play out in real life quite the way I had seen it on TV. No dreamy doctor stepped in and magically sucked the poison from my stomach with a pump. Instead, I had to face a bunch of seriously pissed-off nurses and a gallon of liquid charcoal.

At that particular moment, I didn't care about the house, I

didn't care about Gretchen, and I didn't care about school — I just wanted my parents to leave. I couldn't handle them looking at me like I was damaged.

They stood at the end of my hospital bed staring at me. Neither one of them said a thing — not to me, or to one another. Usually this would be the point where one of us would say something funny and break the tension. My dad would jump around like a gorilla, or my mom would make fun of one of the nurses. This time, no one said anything.

My father has never really been good at emotional situations. He's great for discussions about metaphysical poetry and seventeenth-century British politics, but tears are outside his skill set. When I was four years old, he picked me up from my babysitter after getting a haircut. The shock of seeing him with short hair upset me so much that I cried for hours. He brought me to go get candy and promised he would never cut his hair again. And he didn't.

As he stood there watching his daughter vomit charcoal, his long white hair pulled back into a ponytail, I could tell that he didn't know what to do. But I didn't want to be responsible for making my parents feel better, and so I asked them to leave. Just leave me alone in the ER to vomit my charcoal in peace.

They nodded. My dad took hold of my big toe, gave it a squeeze, and said, "You gonna be okay, kiddo?"

"Yeah, Daddy, I'll be okay."

He left first. My mother, always one step ahead the situation, said, "What are you going to tell them?"

"Just leave."

My mother was right: Eventually, someone was going to ask

me why I'd done this, and I would have to tell them something. I couldn't tell them the truth. I'd just taken fistfuls of painkillers, and I couldn't even tell the psychiatrist why. If I did, my parents would be homeless. There was no doubt in my mind that their home would be condemned. They might even face criminal charges. So when the doctor came with his clipboard and bored look, I told him in my most vacuous teenager voice that "I was just really sad about my scholarship being revoked."

NINETEEN

"**N**OW, DON'T YOU FEEL SILLY?**"** Dr. Shumacher walked into my hospital room all smiles. He had been my family doctor since my house had burned down ten years earlier.

Dr. Shumacher was a throwback to small-town living. Visits to his office for bouts of bronchitis and inhaler refills were like visiting an affable old uncle — of which I didn't have many; our real extended family was never particularly interested in us. Stethoscope in hand, I would be questioned about my grades and after-school activities and teased about my adolescent love life — of which there was none.

"Yeah, not my brightest moment," I responded. I wondered if he would have done something if he had known why I really swallowed all those pills. Stop seeing my parents, perhaps. Implore my father to get help, again. He had been nervous about my leaving for school. When I came in for my precollege physical, he took my parents aside and asked, "Are you going to be okay when she goes to college?" The question itself wasn't an odd one. My parents went everywhere with me, even after I was old enough to drive myself. But from Dr. Shumacher, it was a different kind of question. He was worried about their anxiety levels and handed them a "just in case" prescription for Xanax to help get them through the first few months of my independence.

I saw my parents sneak in behind the doctor. They had been waiting outside my room, looking for an excuse to enter under friendly terms. I had already told them I didn't want them there, but they knew I would keep up my act in front of company.

"You know, you should enroll at Stony Brook and be a teacher. My daughter Katie is a teacher. She gets summers off, and she's getting married."

"Stony Brook has rolling admissions," my mom chimed in.

"Maybe. I'm still figuring out what I'm going to do this year." I hadn't even started to figure out my life outside of a hospital gown, but the absolute last thing I wanted was to become a teacher or go to school on Long Island.

People were always suggesting I become a teacher. "You'll have your summers off to act" was the usual argument, generally followed by "It's good money and a nice life."

At eighteen, there was only one thing in my life I was sure of: I wanted to be someone else — professionally. Any other job would mean a lifetime of being myself, and who I was wasn't worth much.

"Well, keep it in mind. I could see you as a teacher," Dr. Shumacher said. "I'll come back and check on you tomorrow."

After he left to visit his other hospitalized patients, my mother spoke first, before I could kick her out.

"I just want you to know that we rented an apartment. You never have to go back to the house."

That wasn't what I was expecting.

"Okay," I replied. "When do we move in?"

"Your father and I are moving in September first. You're going to the Netherlands," she said. "I've never travelled, never left the country. I want you to have this. I cashed out an annuity. It will cover this semester, and we'll figure out the rest later."

My mother called Rachel shortly after I'd been admitted to the hospital. I wouldn't let my mother stay with me, but she thought that I might let my best friend, and I think she was afraid to leave me alone in my hospital room.

Rachel was perhaps the only person who didn't tiptoe around me, unsure of what to say or do. She trotted into my hospital room with a blanket and a pillow, pushed two chairs together, and spent each night of my hospital stay curled up on a make-shift bed. When the nurses questioned us, she said she was my sister. People always asked if we were sisters — twins on a couple of occasions — and the nurses seemed to buy our lie. While we both had long hair, blue eyes, and girl-next-door qualities to our appearances, it was our mannerisms that gave people that impression. We dressed alike, had the same vocal inflections, the same style of banter — but I was always hyperaware that I acted more like Rachel than she did me. While I struggled to fit in, Rachel had a way of knowing precisely what to do in any social situation, and I counted on her to teach me how to be whoever was necessary at any given moment.

When doctors came by, or my parents poked their heads in, hoping to be allowed in, she gracefully left my room like she had some other person to visit on the floor. A while later, she would emerge with McDonalds and casually bring up moments from our highlight reel: my first kiss, which she dared me to have with a boy that liked me. I spent the whole time staring at her, eyes wide open, as she tried to pantomime French kissing instructions. Or she'd talk about the time I had stayed home sick from school when we had an AP biology take-home test due. We normally traded off tests, changing a few answers each time to make sure it didn't look like we were cheating. I called the school in my most grown-up voice and said that I was her Aunt Kim and that there was a family emergency and she needed to be pulled out of class. The school secretary put Rachel on the phone, and I relayed the test answers to her before she was due in Dr. Sullivan's class. All the while she made understanding *ohs* and *awws* while filling in her Scantron in front of the front office staff. Or the time we went to TGIFriday's and our waiter was so enamored with her he forgot to bring me my soda or food, until she finally ordered for me.

She had somehow made a week in the hospital, getting blood drawn between psych evaluations, seem like any other sleepover.

I asked Rachel not to tell Anna about my suicide attempt, at least not until I was out of the hospital. I felt stupid and dramatic and didn't want anyone else feeling awkward around me, plus Anna had been spending the summer with her grandmother, and I didn't want her to feel like she had to take me in.

When I left the hospital, I didn't know where to go. I couldn't go back to Rachel's house, and I refused to go back home.

I scheduled as many security guard overnight shifts as I could, and the nights I was off I slept in my car. The 1988 Pontiac Grand Am was my safe place. I was meticulous about its upkeep, vacuuming it daily and changing air fresheners monthly so that it always smelled good. I parked my car in my favorite place each night, Peppermint Park. It was a tiny playground across the street from the restaurant I worked at, the place I went when I wanted to be alone. During the day I would sit in my car watching the kids play, and at night I would swing alone on the swings or curl up in the backseat with the pillow and blanket I kept in the trunk.

My father settled right back into his happy-go-lucky self when I left the hospital, content to chalk up my overdose as something else to forget ever happened. My mother couldn't let it go as easily. She was overly careful and accommodating around me, afraid to touch me or say anything that might be upsetting. They made a practice of stopping into the restaurant for dinner almost every night to make sure I was there, but they never questioned my sleeping arrangements. I told them I would never go back to their house, and so they assumed I was at Rachel's. I didn't want them to know I was sleeping in my car. When they lingered at the front of the restaurant before leaving to say good-bye, I would act extra-peppy and tell them everything was fine.

"I hate that word, *fine*," my mom said. "Whenever you say you're fine I know you're anything but."

My parents sold their house to a friend whose husband did contract work. They sold it for a third of its value under the stipulation that it was "as is" and the new owner's responsibility to clean it out and rip it apart. The couple that bought the house stopped speaking to my parents shortly after realizing what they had taken on, but not before mentioning that when they had gotten to the attic, they found hundreds, maybe thousands of beer cans, a man's clothing, and an old cot.

Someone had been living in our attic.

I'd had a feeling. There was a door that led to the attic right across from my bedroom, and I had heard a voice coming through the cracks in the door once. There was so much stuff — old furniture, boxes of papers, and bags upon bags of god knows what — in the space between the attic and my room that I knew it would take herculean strength to get out of the attic through that door. But our garage didn't lock, and there were stairs straight to the attic from there. I told my mom about the voice, and she said I was probably just hearing the rats.

"You were right. Someone was living in the attic," my mom told me when she heard the news. We were in the middle of moving into their new apartment and the cleanness of it all had washed away much of my recent hatred.

I didn't feel justified. I felt violated. Everything about us was wrong. I could go back to Boston and be the perky girl I had perfected, I could board a plane to the Netherlands and be just another American looking for adventure, and when I graduated I could be any number of people, but it didn't matter where I was, or who I pretended to be. I would always be the girl who grew up in garbage.

TWENTY

JUST LIKE AFTER THE FIRE, my family started over
completely after my suicide attempt. New clothes, new furniture, new appliances, new life. Just like after the fire, clean
carpets and new stuff were enough to make me believe that we
wouldn't waste this second second chance.

The apartment still smelled like fresh paint when I left for the
airport less than a week after we moved in. My parents drove me
up to Boston and waited with me in the airport for my flight to
Amsterdam to board.

At the airport, while my father seemed contentedly distracted
by his simultaneous reading of the newspaper and listening to
the news on his pocket radio, my mother took me aside.

"Promise me that you'll never settle. I've settled for so much
in my life because I didn't think I was worth anything," she told
me. "I want you to enjoy this trip, and when you get back, we'll
take out loans for school. We'll make it work."

"I won't let you take out loans for school," I said. "But we'll
make it work."

. . .

Over the course of a month I had gone from living with fleas, rats, and a squatter to living in a castle. Emerson owned a four-teenth-century medieval castle in the southeast of the Nether-lands, complete with two moats and a tower where the village used to slaughter virgins to ward off dragons.

The program director, an Indonesian woman who had lived in the Netherlands long enough to pull off a guttural Dutch ac-cent like a native, plied us with coffee to help keep us awake dur-ing our postflight tour. She showed us around the outer castle — where we would have our classes, where meals would be served, and which housed the ever-important vending machines — as well as the inner castle, where the library and community rooms were located. The town consisted of a bar, the Vink; a post of-fice that was also the convenience store, where we could buy bus tickets called *strippenkart* to take us to the neighboring villages; a bank; a grocery store; and a bakery. The whole town was no more than a mile around.

While many of my fellow students were housed in makeshift dorm rooms, my two roommates and I found ourselves in what once must have been a master bedroom. Untouched by colle-giate renovations, our room was huge, with ornate wallpaper, high ceilings, giant windows overlooking the inner moat, and an inactive fireplace. I had certainly moved up in the housing department.

I changed my class schedule before I left New York, deciding to focus on more academic courses while studying abroad than I did in Boston. I took the one mandatory acting class needed for my major, taught by an eccentric French woman named So-phie who commuted to the Netherlands once a week to direct the class to roll around on the floor and channel our inner ani-mals. The rest of my schedule was filled with history courses. I was in my first class of the semester, the World Since 1914, when the program director knocked on the door and had a word with our teacher. Class ended abruptly and we were ushered to the community room. CNN was on, and we all gathered around it instinctually. There was a fire in the World Trade Center, or at least that's what I thought, until a moment later when I saw a plane hit one of the Twin Towers.

We spent two days crowding around the two telephones in the castle, taking turns calling home and trying to get through the busy lines. I knew my parents were okay where they were — they weren't anywhere near the city — but I was desperate to hear their voices. I had been so angry at my parents before I left, for Gretchen, for the guy in the attic, for the years of living with rats and sludge and fleas, for freezing-cold winter nights, for the years of being left to fend for myself during their alternating depressions, and the years of lying. But in that moment, I only wanted to be home with them. I wanted to tell them how sorry I was that I had hurt them, but how glad I was that they were out of our house — that I would have swallowed a million pills if it meant keeping them from ever living that way again.

"We're okay, honey," my mom said when I finally got through. "I want you to stay in Europe. Apply to a school somewhere in England or Ireland; I don't want you coming back here."

My dad picked up the phone. "Hey, kiddo, you doin' okay over there?"

I didn't say all those things I had wanted to say. I said "I'm fine," told them that I loved them, and went back to my room.

. . .

The rest of the semester went along as planned, sort of. Our advisors told us to avoid telling anyone we were American, to claim we were Canadians whenever possible, since no one hates Canadians. American flags were removed from the front of our dorms, and organized trips were cancelled so that we could travel innocuously. My friends and I still spent our weekends sleeping on trains and travelling from one country to the next, but we were all homesick. Many of my classmates flew home for Thanksgiving, but my two roommates and I went to Rome instead.

There was champagne and chocolates waiting for us in our hotel room. Normally we considered sleeping in a hostel a splurge, but a friend of ours from Emerson worked his way through college as a concierge and arranged for us to stay at the InterContinental for the holiday. We had just spent three days on the island of Ischia and had challenged ourselves to eat nothing but the fruit that grew there — the champagne went straight to our heads.

Our first stop was a Gustav Klimt exhibit at Galleria Nazionale d'Arte Moderna, then a stroll through the cat-filled streets of Rome, until we stumbled into a little trattoria on a cobblestone street. Our waiter loved Americans and plied us with wine and shots of lemon-flavored liquor, all while serenading us with what we assumed was opera but could just as well have been the Italian equivalent of "Row, Row, Row Your Boat."

We stumbled to the subway and climbed the Spanish Steps to our hotel, where I tried to sober up enough to call my family. My efforts were futile — my parents promptly put me on speakerphone and let the whole family listen in on my drunken Thanksgiving salutations. The whole world seemed to be in mourning, but I was more thankful than I had ever been. My family had survived itself, and I was full of limoncello.

TWENTY-ONE

FTER RETURNING TO BOSTON from the Netherlands, I cashed in my trust at a steep penalty and took on another job, balancing waitressing, babysitting, and secretarial work before, between, and after classes. I added a minor in marketing communications, realizing that I would possibly need a backup plan one day, and an acting degree wasn't going to do me any favors when it came to the hefty student loans I was taking on.

I spent my summers in Boston, too, working and taking as many summer classes as I could because they were cheaper in the long run. By the time my twentieth birthday rolled around, I had stockpiled enough credits to graduate. I didn't need a senior year, and so I didn't have one.

The only collegiate requirement I had left was an internship of my choosing. I chose to work for a talent agency in Los Angeles. In late August, I packed up what few belongings I had in Boston and boarded a plane to LAX. The school had arranged for me to live in a two-bedroom apartment in North Hollywood with two other Emersonians and a student from Boston University. We got along well but didn't spend all that much time together, each of us testing the waters of LA in our own way — one was an actress, another an amateur skydiver considering a career as a stunt double, and the girl from BU was looking to work her way into the business side of the music industry. Our pleasantly sterile apartment wasn't far from the Hollywood sign, and was directly across the street from the Universal lot.

My mother had been, for the first time in my life, completely unsupportive of my decision to move to Los Angeles. She was afraid that I would fall in love with the West Coast and never come home again. It was a valid fear, because for the first time in my life, everything that could go right for me did.

I had taken the promise I made my mother seriously, making a mantra out of *never settle*, repeating the two words in my head over and over again when I wasn't sure whether to do the smart thing or the scary thing. *Never settle* echoed on and on in my head during the days I was locked in a closet sorting headshots, a requirement of my internship at the agency. I questioned other interns about possible upgrades in responsibilities, and after realizing there weren't any, I didn't settle: I quit my internship after one week and went back to submitting my résumé to casting directors. The production team for a show being filmed on the Universal lot right across the street from my apartment needed an intern to help schedule appointments and run auditions. I wouldn't be taking the entertainment industry by storm, but the women in the casting office were nice, and nice was better than being locked in a closet.

When I told my aunt Lee about my internship, she put me in touch with the wife of her former personal trainer. He had stopped training Lee a few years earlier after his wife took a VP job in Universal's marketing department and the family moved to LA. I called her office and was welcomed over for a talk and a tour.

If she weren't a public relations guru, this film studio executive could have been a movie star; she looked like a younger, blonder Annette Bening. I did my best to impress her, sharing practiced speeches about my minor and being an active member of the Public Relations Student Society of America. I told her I was considering a career in PR after my internship was over. I wasn't sure if that was the truth, but it wasn't necessarily a lie either. College had been my ultimate goal for the majority of my life, and now that it was coming to an end, I had no idea what was next for me. I did know that I wanted to be polished, poised, and respected like this amazing woman who had allowed me to steal a moment of her very important life.

She took me out to lunch the following week, introduced me to people I should have known but didn't, and told me to call her when my internship was over to see about a job.

My internship was going equally well — the casting director let me read with auditioning actors, introduced me to the show's main cast, and even cast me in an episode to help me get my SAG card. I'd lucked into a few days of bit-part work on TV shows my parents dutifully taped back in New York. Since I wasn't auditioning, I suspected my boss had pulled a few strings to help me, but she never brought it up, and so neither did I.

Beautiful people everywhere seemed to be welcoming me into their fold, offering me sunshine and jobs, farmers' markets and craft services — it was all so easy, and easy was never the life I expected. I didn't know what to do with easy except to poke and prod at it, looking for disappointment.

I found a comfortable discomfort in loneliness. My supervisors were kind to me, but they didn't exactly want to hang out with me on the weekends, and I found the endless conversations about the entertainment industry among my peer group to be utterly mind-numbing. The people I loved, the people I trusted to simply be myself around, were all on the East Coast.

I hadn't made any friends outside of my roommate social circle, and we were acquaintances at best. Every couple of weeks we would venture out to a bar to scope out the scene. I was still underage, but within days of my arrival, Rachel had sent a care package with a driver's license and two credit cards she didn't use in case I was asked for backup ID. Armed as "Rachel," I stood awkwardly around Burbank bars, wondering if all of the people inside would end up driving home drunk, ordering Midori sours because they looked pretty, and excusing myself to the bathroom any time a guy approached me.

Romance seemed to me like foolishness, reserved for people with nothing better to do; I had gone through the entirety of college without a single date and I didn't plan on starting here, especially since I wasn't sure I wanted to stay in LA.

Moving back to New York after college meant moving back in with my parents for the first time since we had left the house behind. I loved them, their visits to Boston, and even the brief visits home I made for the holidays, but I wasn't sure if I could go back to living their way of life. When they picked me up from the airport after my semester in the Netherlands, their new apartment was spotless. It had been less than six months since I had tried to kill myself, and my mother diligently picked up every stray paper, portable radio, or dish that was put down for more than a few minutes at a time, afraid of my reaction. But in the two years since, the trauma behind their move faded, and so did their diligence. My mother started paying me a warning call before I came home. "Don't expect too much," she liked to say before launching into a long tirade about how hard it was to live with my father, as if living with him was something I knew nothing about. She would tell me she had been cleaning for days but making little impact on his ever-growing collection. It was the same speech before every visit, and I knew it wasn't just him at fault. She was still quite the shopper. Instead of TV shopping shows, she could now ward off boredom by shopping online. The combination of the two of them was too much for the small apartment to handle.

I got lucky when the show I interned for was cancelled in December. I considered it a get-out-of-LA-free card. I'd stick around until shooting wrapped, and afterward I could move back to New York having tried and failed through no fault of my own. After two years of convincing myself that I never wanted to go back home again, I was actually excited to be with my family — despite my mother's preflight warning call.

"I just don't want you to hate me when you see it," she said. "I made sure the door to your bedroom is always closed so nothing sneaks in there." I could hear the shame in her voice and the fear, as if she thought I would come home, take one look at their apartment, and slit my wrists.

"It's okay, Mom. I'll help you clean up." There was no point in making her feel worse by telling her I was disappointed. It's nothing I hadn't experienced before.

When I made it home after my flight, the two-bedroom apartment was worse than I had expected. My father's papers had taken over the entire loveseat and two thirds of the couch in the living room — that was his "office," he said, as if bus drivers everywhere needed an office to sort their timesheets and behavioral reports on second graders. There was a thin pathway between his wall of papers and the television that allowed us to walk through the apartment from the kitchen to the bedrooms, but no one but my father could actually sit down and watch a movie in the stuffed sitting area.

My mother had a wall in their bedroom that consisted of her computer desk and boxes of things she had ordered online but hadn't found use for or time to return. If she wasn't in the kitchen cooking something, she was there, sitting at the computer with her back to the rest of the house.

Piles of clothes took over the top of their dresser, and my father's side of the bed consisted of bags and bags of papers. The kitchen fared better than the rest of the house. There were still some parts of the floor visible, and the kitchen table was kept half-cleared so that we could at least eat as a family if we sat close together. My room, as my mother had promised, was spotless, just as I'd left it the last time I visited them.

I told myself that the apartment was fine; we could cook food, the heating worked, and showers could be had any time of the day. I couldn't ask for more.

TWENTY-TWO

MY MOTHER HAD WALKED RIGHT past me when I got off the plane. I had lost almost twenty pounds while in LA, and she didn't recognize me. The weight loss wasn't a conscious effort — I had simply stopped eating because no one I knew ate, and so I felt silly sitting down to a meal when a Diet Coke seemed to be enough to sustain the people around me for days on end.

In my first few days at home, I made up for every meal I had skipped while in Los Angeles. As soon as I finished one plate, my mother was standing by with another. With me home, she seemed to have found a purpose in life — making up for lost mothering. She was happier than I'd seen her in years, spending hours in the kitchen preparing meals she hadn't made since I was a child. I didn't remember my mother loving to cook — it always seemed like an annoying task she had to do at the end of a long commute.

If I strayed from her eyesight for more than a few minutes at a time, she would call out for me to make sure I hadn't disappeared. Not that I could go anywhere. I didn't have a car, which meant I was completely homebound during the day while my father was at work. I wasn't used to having to be accounted for, having someone else doing my laundry or cooking for me. I missed the ordered life I had created for myself, but it was obvious that she needed to do this, and so I spent hours eating, being within earshot, and letting my mother take care of me.

My father seemed less fazed with my return. I was gone and now I was back, and his routine stayed the same: He went to work in the morning and came home in the evening. Once home, he would sit on the couch, turn on the radio, and proceed to inspect the various documents he surrounded himself with, ignoring my mother and me.

He shifted magazines, pens, and the portable cassette players he carried with him to work (so that he could record the thoughts and musings that entered his head while driving) to the floor to make room for me on the couch one night that first week.

"What are these papers on the coffee table?"

"What, this?" he said, gesturing to the papers piled six inches high. "Your mom won't let me get a desk and a bookcase."

"Why do you need a desk and a bookcase?"

"So I can organize my work."

"Do you think you'd be able to keep the rest of the house clean if you had a desk and a bookcase, Daddy?" I tried to imagine what kind of desk would suit my father's needs. Based on the hundreds of plastic bags filled with papers that covered the couches, tables, floors, and closets, we would be looking at a pretty gigantic desk.

"Absolutely. No doubt about it," he said.

"Okay, I'll talk to Mom about it."

"Thanks, kiddo. You're okay, I don't care what your mother says about you," he said, laughing.

I left him to his photocopied articles, highlighters, and old PC magazines, and went to talk to my mom. She was at her computer, and because she had started to lose much of her vision to macular degeneration, the type size she used to read emails could be seen across the room.

"I was talking to Dad," I said. "He says that he could contain his papers better if he had a desk and a bookcase."

"I'm sure he did. That's his latest argument."

"Maybe we should get them for him."

She looked at me as if she was reassessing my intelligence. "There aren't enough desks and bookcases in the world to contain your father."

"But isn't it worth a try?"

"We've tried. He's had desks and bookcases. Kim, he had a whole house and he filled it — do you really think three drawers are going to fix him?"

I did and I didn't. I hadn't quite given up on finding the key to fixing him, but to be honest, it hadn't been on my mind much in the last couple of years. I didn't bring it up again, and hoped that my father hadn't gotten too excited about the prospect of office furniture.

It didn't take long, maybe a month, for me to stop seeing the mess. Life had returned to normal.

My graduation present was $3,000 and the instructions to buy myself a car. I felt guilty taking that kind of money from my parents. If anyone needed a new car, it was them. They were driving a hand-me-down Bronco that was only a pothole away from being scrap metal. The passenger-side window didn't close, and my mother would come home from trips to the store with chapped lips and ruddy cheeks from the winter breeze hitting her in the face on the way home. The seatbelts had been cut off by the previous owners, and the power steering didn't work; my father swayed with each corner the car took, putting the whole of his weight into turning the steering wheel. I needed a car, but only in the short term. I gave myself a six-month deadline to get out of Long Island, time enough to save up for a security deposit and a few months' rent in New York City. I would get the best car I could find for $3,000 and give it to my parents as soon as I could save enough money to move out.

I put Rachel's boyfriend Tim in charge of my car search; he knew cars better than anyone I knew, and I trusted him with my money, for the most part. I was a little nervous when he said he'd found a great deal on a practically brand-new Kia that had less than 5,000 miles on it and was only $2,400 — for the moment, at least, because it was listed for auction on eBay.

My mother and I scoured the car's Internet listing, searching for hidden accident reports, but the whole thing looked aboveboard. "It has airbags," my mom said. "I'd like to know you'll be safe."

"This coming from the woman that needs aviator goggles in her own car," I fired back.

"Yes, but I'm your mother. It's my job to worry about you."

She had no idea how much I worried about her and my father.

We bid, we won, and we drove to Queens to pick up my new car. Tim was right: The car was in great condition, far better than most of the cars my parents had driven in my lifetime, which only made me feel more guilty about the extravagance of the gift.

With a car, I could finally get a job, but the restaurant I had worked at during high school and my first summer home from college had closed, and the only place hiring in the dead of winter was a Ruby Tuesday near my parents' apartment. Shortly after I started, I realized why the HELP WANTED sign taped on the front door looked withered and sun-bleached — it was a permanent fixture. During my first shift, two servers quit, and another was caught selling drugs in the bathroom — she wasn't fired, they needed her on the floor. If I were lucky, I would come home with forty dollars in tips after a weekend of waitressing. Even with my housing paid for, I didn't make nearly enough money to save for my future life. With what little I made, I filled my gas tank, subscribed to *Backstage*, and paid my student loans, and barely had enough left over to meet Rachel and Tim a couple nights a week. They were still in college, but they'd gone to school close to home, which meant I had a modicum of a social life — although it usually consisted of disco fries at 2 a.m.

Because I lived in the suburbs, my copy of *Backstage* always came a few days late, meaning that half of the open calls listed inside were already long over, so I stuck with mail-order submissions for acting jobs. I never wanted to be an ingénue — sweet girls-next-door with dreams of falling in love, perhaps tap-dancing a little, who had a happy ending never appealed to me. In college, when I was responsible for coming up with my own scenes and monologues for class, I was drawn to the toenail-chewing hillbillies, cheerful sociopaths, and quirky outcasts — people who would never quite fit in, whether they knew it or not. People I understood.

That was fine for college, but after weeks with no responses to my submissions, I came to terms with the fact that my headshots looked how I looked in real life: like a sweet girl-next-door with dreams of falling in love, perhaps tap-dancing a little, who would have a happy ending. That was who I was going to get called in to play.

Within days of dropping my first batch of submissions for lovelorn young women in the mail, I got a call to audition for *The Importance of Being Earnest.*

I did my best to ask about the audition details in the most professional of tones, mimicking the agents I'd spoken to as a casting intern. "What should I have prepared? By when do you plan on making a decision?" After I hung up, I realized I had absolutely no idea what I was doing and I had no idea where I was going. The theater was in Brooklyn. The only thing I knew about Brooklyn was which rappers hailed from there.

I was scared of driving into Brooklyn, scared of going on my first real audition, scared of being outed as someone who foolishly thought that she could make a career as an actor.

I went to the kitchen, where my mother was chopping onions, to ask her to go on my first job interview with me.

"You're not serious," was her response.

"I'm nervous, and I've never driven in Brooklyn."

"Why would you take a role you have to drive to Brooklyn for?"

"Because it's a role."

"Kim," she said. "Fine."

· · ·

I pulled up to the theater an hour late for my audition. I'd taken a wrong turn off of the Brooklyn-Queens Expressway and been too nervous to ask for directions. I tiptoed into the theater and prepared to apologize profusely in hopes that I'd still be allowed to read for one of the two female leads. My mom waited in the car, in January, to preserve what little dignity I was pretending to have.

The theater was nothing more than a large storefront with a curtain separating the stage from the waiting area. The director popped his head out, asked who I was, and motioned with his finger for me to wait. From the plywood bench lining the bright blue hallway, I could hear each perfectly posh-accented word the girl auditioning inside the theater said. I made a mental note about how she was delivering her lines so as to not read mine the same way. The actress walked out trailed by the two men holding the audition, each competing to say good-bye last.

Men, in general, did not fall all over themselves for me, at least not that I'd ever noticed, so I was pretty sure my chances of getting a part were slim. Still, I had to start somewhere, and I walked into the theater as if I were someone who actually possessed a spine.

"Hi, I'm Kimberly Rae Miller. Sorry I'm late."

"We were wondering where you were. Not a problem. There are two sets of sides — Gwendolyn and Cecily, and we'll start with Gwendolyn." The director handed me two sets of stapled photocopies, starting immediately on his cue.

Every acting class I'd ever taken in my life meant nothing — I was making every mistake I could. I tried to play coy, but instead started walking around in circles on the stage. I never looked up from the page, too scared that I'd forget a word or accidentally look my auditioner in the eye. And the accent I had carefully practiced around the house in the days preceding the audition kept fading in and out.

When I was finished with Gwendolyn, they let me read for Cecily, and when I was finished butchering Cecily's lines, they asked if I had a Shakespeare monologue to audition for their production of *A Midsummer Night's Dream*.

I didn't, so I declined the offer to extend my torture. Just as they'd done with the pretty girl before me, the two men in the theater followed me out, doing their best to outflirt one another. I didn't think I had a chance in hell of getting a part, but I was actually feeling okay about my first audition.

A few days later, as I left my shift at Ruby Tuesday having made an astronomical eight dollars in tips, I got a call. I got a part. I got *the* part. I was going to be Cecily Cardew, the most sweet and maniacal of ingénues.

I was so excited I didn't give a second thought to the fact that I would be spending the next two months going back and forth to that very sketchy Brooklyn theater. Personal safety was of little consequence, because I was now officially a working actress — albeit not one who was actually getting paid.

When I got home, I shared my news and asked my mom to come with me to every audition. She politely declined.

The first rehearsal was in late January, and I immediately recognized one of my cast members: The girl ahead of me at the audition was playing the other female lead, Gwendolyn. Just as I'd done in middle school, I studied her for clues as how to behave during a table reading.

I started to ease up a bit when people around the table chuckled as I delivered Cecily's lines. Maybe winning the role hadn't been a fluke.

Over the course of our rehearsals, Cecily rubbed off on me more and more. Gwendolyn and I giggled through rehearsals, daring each other to interject Oscar Wilde's carefully drafted dialogue with modern vernacular to test our director's attention level. Perhaps it was the flirtatious nature of the play — or perhaps, for the first time in my life, I had nothing better to occupy my mind — but I even found myself with a crush: a certain butler who caught my eye.

The only problem was that staring was the only way we seemed to connect. I had nicknamed him Creepy Guy to Rachel and Tim when I recounted how he spent our hours in rehearsal staring at me, only to sit next to me and not say anything at all.

It was creepy, but also kind of cute. I'd never rendered anyone speechless before. I would listen in when he spoke to other members of the cast — he was usually talking incessantly about his time spent in Cuba and would break into Spanish whenever he could. I thought he was Jewish, but what did I know? Maybe Cubans looked Jewish.

I didn't really know how to flirt, but I knew how to read, and in an effort to actually get him to speak to me, I hit the bookstore. The small, musty bookstore in town was lacking in works by Cuban authors, but I could at least demonstrate a love of Latin culture with a copy of *One Hundred Years of Solitude.* I brought it to every rehearsal and I never missed an opportunity between scenes to read it quietly in hopes of catching his eye. My plan finally paid off when he struck up a conversation about the book.

. . .

Turns out Paul *was* Jewish and not Cuban in the slightest. He grew up among Washington, D.C.'s elite; his father owned a law firm, and Paul had gone to high school with Chelsea Clinton and played on the football team with Al Gore Jr. Paul had about as opposite of an upbringing from me as you could get.

I started spending more and more time with him in Brooklyn. Paul's apartment wasn't far from the theater. I realized on our strolls back to his place after rehearsal that Park Slope wasn't exactly dangerous territory, but every bit the yuppie stomping ground that Beacon Hill was to me in Boston. Two avenues from the theater, there were designer boutiques, French cafés, and dog parks.

When the run of *Earnest* came to an end, the Reverend Chasuble, whose offstage name was Seamus, told me his roommate was moving out in June. He lived six blocks from the theater. The rent of the two-bedroom apartment with a backyard in Park Slope was $600 per person per month. I'd been scouring Craigslist looking for housing, but everything was out of my price range. I could maybe afford $600 a month — if I got a better paying part-time job. I had four months to save up the $1,200 needed to move in.

I already had my next role lined up. The director of *Earnest* had asked me to step into the role of Titania in his production of *A Midsummer Night's Dream* after the woman he'd originally cast had quit unexpectedly. Since I'd been spending most of my time in the city anyway, I started sending my headshots to restaurants instead of theaters. I was slowly learning that restaurants in New York were even pickier than some casting directors, requiring extensive serving résumés and a look to match the décor of the dining room. It was finally an upscale bistro in Tribeca that liked my look. They didn't have any waitressing positions, but a hostess position was open. I would have to wear tight black clothing, make sure my hair and makeup were perfect, and treat the posh clientele like old and better-than-me friends.

I could do that. I made better money hostessing in Tribeca than I ever had as a waitress and squirreled all of my earnings away for my upcoming move.

My life wasn't glamorous, but it was working out perfectly.

TWENTY-THREE

I WAS FULLY UNPACKED and decorated in less than an hour. The girlishness of my bedroom, with its white rod-iron bedframe and a pastel purple-and-green quilt, was a stark contrast to the rest of the apartment, which was decidedly more masculine.

The only windows in the first-floor apartment were in the bedrooms, and the living room and kitchen had a cavelike quality that was only exacerbated by the dark oriental rug Seamus had placed in the living room and large wooden masks his mother, who was an art dealer, had given him after a trip to Africa. Signs with catchy slogans like "Smokin' One" and old Guinness ads were located around the apartment, and a painting of Mao Zédōng hung in the entryway.

Paul quickly started referring to me as Mao, despite the fact that the painting wasn't mine. "It's perfect for you," he said. "You both have five-year plans." I found comfort in organization, and shortly after I'd moved home from LA had decided on a series of goals to build a life around. I had made my plan into Power-Point slides categorized by career, family, finance, and personal life goals, which I then converted into a screensaver for my computer — a regular reminder that there was work to be done. Each time my computer was left unattended for too long, I was reminded of my goals to pay off 10 percent of my student loans each year, get my Equity Card, visit my parents once a month, start a retirement account, and hit the gym five days a week.

While Seamus and I split the rent evenly, I had the bigger bedroom with the bigger window, and he had the door to the backyard. Since he was an avid gardener, that seemed to suit him just fine, and I reaped the benefits of his green thumb when he stocked the kitchen with more fresh herbs and vegetables than either of us could eat.

We got along, but we weren't close friends. He worked days while I worked nights, and we were rarely home at the same time.

As a housewarming present, Rachel gave me a small watercolor painting of a neat little cottage floating in a watery green field. "This reminded me of you," she said, and I knew what she meant. When we had talked about our dreams when we were kids, long before she and Anna had started putting the pieces of my family's situation together, I had told her that all I wanted one day was a little home that was only mine — just a small space that I could keep neat. The apartment was Seamus's through and through, but my bedroom was my cottage. I hung the painting next to my bedroom door so that I could look at it each time I left and remind myself that I was finally becoming who I had always wanted to be.

Shortly after I moved to Brooklyn, my parents announced that they were also moving. Their rent was facing a steep increase, and they had found a slightly cheaper, slightly newer, slightly bigger apartment in a development a few miles away from where I grew up.

The move sounded perfect, with one catch: The new development had regular apartment inspections. Every couple of months, someone from the development's management company would take a walk through each apartment to make sure that the tenants were taking care of the property, that the smoke and carbon dioxide detectors were working, and that tenants weren't hiding any unapproved pets on their premises. My parents considered this to be a huge invasion of privacy, but I thought that these regular inspections might just be the pressure they needed to keep their house in order.

The one thing standing between my parents and their next clean slate was the mess they were still living in. Packing hadn't been an issue for their last two moves, between the fire and simply abandoning their home with everything in it. They seemed to be completely oblivious to the fact that they couldn't just show up to this next apartment and fill it with clothes and furniture later. My mother asked me to come out to Long Island on the weekends to help them prepare for the move. I didn't know how to explain to Paul why my parents seemed to need so much help — months of help — so I used my mother's failing vision as an excuse for my constant trips home.

"She's going blind" wasn't an excuse that was easy to question, and Paul never did, but he hinted that he felt like I abandoned him each weekend for the comforts of home.

Once I got home, cleaning and packing seemed to be the last thing on anyone's mind. There was always something that needed to be picked up from a store, something on television that needed to be watched, a new restaurant that needed trying, or an article that needed reading. Weekend after weekend, I would declare that I wouldn't clean unless they cleaned, and weekend after weekend I would go back to Brooklyn having done absolutely nothing. I had mistakenly believed that as moving day loomed closer my parents would stop procrastinating and start packing, but when I came home the weekend of the move everything was exactly where it had always been — everywhere.

My father carried on as usual, stationed on his worn couch cushion, surrounded by paper, but my mother had hidden herself in the corner of her bedroom, alternating between the one foot of space between her bed and computer desk, and pretending to sleep when I came in to check on her. She didn't want to shop or leave the bedroom to cook. She had become catatonic in her fear.

"We're never going to get this done," she said, before breaking down into tears. "I don't know where to start."

"One box at a time," I told her. "If you pack what you want, I'll clean up what's left."

Overwhelmed and uninterested, my parents had two days left on their lease, and I realized that they weren't just procrastinating — they *couldn't* face their mess. It had been so easy for me to slip right back into tiptoeing around boxes, bags, and broken things when I'd moved home, and this was their everyday. If they couldn't differentiate between trash and treasure, at least I could, so I grabbed a garbage bag.

That was enough to get their attention. Every plastic bag of papers that went into the garbage was immediately retrieved by my father.

"Do you know what's in that?"

"Paper," I told him. It was only paper.

"You can't just throw things out without looking at them," he scolded.

"Fine, leave it all here and let the management company throw it out," I said, before storming into my bedroom and giving up on my parents.

My resolve only lasted until morning, when I kicked my parents out of their own apartment.

"*Go* — go shopping, go to a movie, go anywhere, but leave me alone!" I yelled.

"We need to pack," my mother said, as if she'd been waiting all along for this exact moment.

"That's what I'm doing."

My father fiddled with his coat, waiting for my mother to make a definitive decision for the both of them.

"Okay, we'll be back in a couple of hours and then we'll get started," my mom said. "Call us when you want us to bring you lunch."

My parents left before I could change my mind, and I was left to figure out how to clean and pack their piles before the movers came the next day.

When my parents had first moved into the apartment, they had been so excited for me to finally invite Rachel and Anna over. At eighteen years old, I could finally have a sleepover. But in the years since, they had returned to greeting them from behind a crack in the door. Rachel hadn't been inside the apartment for years, but I needed the help, and for the first time I could remember, I didn't care about embarrassing my parents.

She and Anna knew about what went on in my house. I didn't have to tell them — they'd figured it out over the years of corner drop-offs, requests to shower at their houses after school, and walks to my parents' junk-filled car — but this was the first time I was letting either of them see what it was really like. When Rachel knocked, I was already covered in cobwebs and bird dander. I opened the door wide, giving her a good look at what she was getting into, in case she wanted to back out.

"Hey, hon," she said, taking a look around. "Are your parents here?"

"No, I sent them out, but they'll probably come home and start hovering soon."

"What should I do?"

We started by throwing out all of the bags of papers my father had out in the open, then we started hunting for the strategically hidden bags. I was sure there was some sort of method behind my father's filing system, but I didn't have the time to go through each bag to find out. I knew I was throwing away important documents. Unpaid bills, uncashed checks, medical records, and work documents were all hidden amid the store circulars, yellowed newspapers, and half-filled notebooks. But as far as I was concerned they were all just paper, and there was always more paper.

Under the coffee table, my father kept a graveyard of broken radios and sole-flapping sneakers. The wires and shoelaces tangled together, creating one solid mass of things my father would fix one day. I threw it all out. I threw out boxes from Home Shopping Club, QVC, and Amazon, even with their contents still safely guarded in plastic.

My parents called midway through the day to see if they could bring me food, but I told them to stay out, that I would order pizza. I couldn't afford the time delay that managing their feelings would create.

My mother paused when I told her Rachel was helping. "Okay, then — tell her I say hi."

Stiff, stained clothing was found under tables and chairs, on the bottom of closets, and under the bed. There was no point in washing them, so they went, too.

Unmarked VHS tapes — many with my old dance recitals, school plays, and the bit parts I had done while I was in Los Angeles recorded on them — went in the trash. I had no use for nostalgia if it took up space.

We boxed their towels and linens, cooking supplies and shoes; vacuumed carpets that hadn't been visible in two years; mopped stained linoleum; and scrubbed the bathtub until it looked like it had been clean all along.

There were hundreds of unused toiletries: enough shampoo, conditioner, body wash, toothpaste, and deodorant to keep the South Shore of Long Island shower-fresh for the rest of the decade.

Cans of expired beans, sauces, and soups took over the kitchen cupboards — my mother was convinced that expiration dates were just a ploy to make you throw out perfectly good food. They went in the garbage. I refused to touch the refrigerator. Full to the brim, only the front had food still edible. The rest had been pushed to the back and forgotten, creating a familiar soupy mess in the vegetable and deli bins that brought back memories I was trying incredibly hard to keep at bay.

The walls and couch cushions were stained and the flooring spotty, but the apartment was clean and packed by the time my parents came home around midnight.

"Wow, you girls did a great job," my mother said.

I didn't say anything. I couldn't say anything. I was so angry with them for living this way again.

Rachel, socially adept as always, took over, talking to my mother about her plans for grad school and her summer job working as a dockmaster on Fire Island.

I watched my father look for some sign of his papers, under couch cushions or in coat pockets. Something to find comfort in.

After Rachel left, the questions started coming.

"Where did you put my box of old Day-Timers?"

"I hope you didn't throw out my ice-cream maker, it only needed one part to work again."

I didn't say anything.

"Oh, you're not talking to us," my mom said as if I were seven years old again and being adorably rebellious.

"I'm not not talking," I said. "The refrigerator still needs cleaning."

TWENTY-FOUR

THE FRESHLY LAID CARPET and recently painted walls of the new apartment were enough to make me forget why I was so angry — again.

My parents didn't have all that much furniture. They trashed their full-length sofa because it had become worn and misshapen from years of my father's bags weighing down on it. The loveseat fared better, and my father immediately took up shop there, creating for himself a new space to inspect whatever documentation the world sent his way.

With their bedroom furniture, loveseat, and dining room table in place, the rest of their life was deemed unworthy of unpacking, or was just left boxed up "for the next move." They hadn't even slept a night in their new home, but they were already deciding whether it was worth settling in.

The walls of the guest room — my room — were lined with those boxes, filled with bedroom and bathroom linens, decorative candles and knickknacks given as gifts and therefore deemed nonpurgeable, and family photos. My mother didn't like making holes in the walls, she said, so pictures were framed but never hung, and usually ended up buried or stepped on. They were better off in boxes.

"Do you think Paul would like to come out for a weekend?" my mother asked before I left for the city. My parents had met Paul briefly after they'd come to see us in *Earnest*. Bringing a boyfriend home for the weekend seemed way too normal, the kind of thing that regular, run-of-the-mill clean people did without a second thought. I knew I could blame whatever mess was around on the recent move, and figured the sooner the better in regard to getting a family visit over with.

Paul was immediately enamored with my father.

"Your dad is brilliant," he said, as he curled up next to me on the futon in the guest room. The two had sat together for hours on the small loveseat in the living room, my father simultaneously listening to NPR and reciting the contents of any related reports he had listened to earlier in the day, week, month, or his lifetime.

"I know." It was so easy to take my father's incessant babbling about forty years' worth of news and social commentary for granted, and often when he spoke on end about the British rule of Rhodesia, or comparisons of medical care in social democracies, I zoned out. In Paul, he had an eager audience. Paul himself was no dummy; he often bragged that his brain was worth a half-million dollars, the sum of tuition for the elite private school education he'd had since childhood. Despite his pricey brain, he had decided to become the disciple of an eccentric old Russian acting teacher, and with a few exceptions like the show we met doing, he spent his time developing performance art pieces with her.

"He's just like your father," my mom said. "Brilliant and completely devoid of ambition."

The idea of finding a man like my father didn't scare me. Paul wasn't a collector of anything — he could be messy, but was mostly just a normal guy when it came to housekeeping. His brilliance and determination to be exactly who he was, despite social expectation, were things I admired in him, and in my father.

But sharing an intellect and sense of self wasn't enough to win my father over. Like my mother, my father wasn't a big fan of Paul, which was odd, because for the most part my father was a fan of everyone.

"I think you're too young to be dating someone so seriously," he told me over tea and the politics section while Paul was in the shower. I couldn't imagine another father encouraging his twenty-one-year-old daughter to play the field, and I had a feeling his comment wasn't so much about my age, but about Paul himself. There was something about my boyfriend that my parents didn't like. I wasn't sure if it was parental instinct or perhaps a sense that they were losing me kicking in, but I wasn't planning to give up the only normal thing in my life.

A few weeks after visiting my parents, Paul and I took a bus to Washington, D.C., so that I could meet his. The first stop on the family bonding tour was the FDR Memorial. Paul and his father immediately broke off to catch up, leaving me with Paul's mother. While I tried to make conversation about the Great Depression, she was more to the point.

"What does your father do, Kimberly?"

I remembered being utterly confused the first time someone queried my father's profession as a means of getting to know me. That was back at Emerson, as my social sphere broadened from my hometown friends who grew up in working-class homes like I did to wealthy children of the entertainment industry elite and captains of industry. There was no confusion now. I knew Paul's mother was judging my social worth.

"He drives a bus."

I didn't pass my first test, and Paul's mother had nothing left to say, so she turned and walked away to find her husband and son, leaving me with President Roosevelt and his copper dog.

Paul's family's home was immense. I'd never been in a house as large as his, and in the center of it all was a sports room that included a full-size football goalpost on one end and a full-size basketball net on the other. A mural of a crowd scene with the family etched into it covered one wall, and hundreds of years' worth of sports paraphernalia lined all the others. Bright-red, purple, and gray walls decorated the rest of the house, and gaudy sculptures in equally bright colors seemed to pop up from out of nowhere. I tried not to leave Paul's side when I visited, afraid I would break something and have to replace it.

Over the next three-and-half years, our relationships with each other's parents only seemed to worsen. My parents started referring to him as "the Little Prince," a nickname he was given when we stopped at a rest stop to use the restrooms on a road trip to a family wedding with my parents. After his trip to the bathroom, Paul ordered a meal at one of the fast-food counters and sat down to eat it, leaving the rest of us in the car thinking he'd had serious business to take care of in the public restroom.

"That boy has entitlement oozing out of his pores," my mother said.

Paul's family didn't even pretend to like me. When I didn't go home with him for Rosh Hashanah one year because I needed to work, his father invited a young, pretty paralegal from his firm to accompany his son to synagogue and family dinners.

Paul started visiting D.C. more often after that. He was trying his hand at regional theater in hopes of qualifying for his Equity Card, he told me. I didn't think much of the trips. I was also balancing an acting career and, at this point, a full-time job in events marketing for a national nonprofit. That was, until I opened up my email inbox one day and found an email from the young, pretty, Rosh Hashanah–going paralegal.

She wrote *I thought you should know* in the subject line and pasted various instant messages and email exchanges she'd had with Paul, most alluding to their sexual relationship.

I had thought I was one of those people who would marry their first love. Paul knew everything about me, including that my father was "a bit messier than most." He knew that I went home every couple of months to clean my parents' apartment before inspection. He knew about the weeklong crying spells that followed, how consuming my need to take care of my parents had become, and how guilty I felt about my anger and disappointment.

I wanted to forgive Paul — not because of my love for him, but because I didn't think anyone else would ever love me enough to accept all the things that were wrong with me.

I sat on the couch watching Paul cry on the carpet. He told me he needed to sleep with her, needed to have a relationship with her, in order to know whether he really wanted to be with me. I knew I was done. Done with Paul, done with romance, done with letting anyone new into my carefully guarded life.

TWENTY-FIVE

I SPENT MY NIGHTS GETTING married, playing the comically naïve bride in an off-Broadway wedding show, asking the most conservative audience members I could find for sex advice, consecrating my love for the actor opposite me with a doughnut wedding ring. After that, I was a cupcake-obsessed Catholic schoolgirl, and after that, a comedienne for hire. I had a lot of fun onstage that year, but I wasn't fulfilling the fantasy I once had of spending night after night in gut-wrenching drama, pushing my emotional capacity to the edge and inspiring people in the audience to reflect on their own lives. I had once had a dream of spending my life performing in socially reflective theater meant to inspire change, like the actors in the Group Theatre had in the 1930s. But that didn't exist in my world, and so my life as an actor meant being really silly.

I had a small group of friends in New York, mostly friends who had started out as Paul's but had stayed close to me after our breakup. Paul's college roommate Aziz and Aziz's girlfriend Becky, along with another of Paul's Brandeis friends, Abby, were the people I got drinks with after work, where I dished about the random unsuccessful dates I would go on. When I wasn't working, I went to Long Island to spend my free time with my parents and with Anna, Rachel, and Tim. Professionally, I felt like I'd gotten about as far up the theatrical food chain as I ever would. When I was still in high school, my acting teacher told me that I should only be an actor if I couldn't think of anything else that I could ever do. At the time, that was true, but I had reached a point where I was looking for something else that might keep me satisfied, at the very least. My quarter-life crisis brought with it LSATs and law school applications. I didn't really think I would get into law school, but it was a fun fantasy.

While I didn't aim particularly high up on the law school hierarchy, I got into all of the second-tier schools I applied to. After work, I would spread out each acceptance letter on my bed and look for some sign in the embossed stationery that the school was right for me.

A few weeks before I had to make my final decision, I got a call from a director. I had stopped auditioning by the time the acceptance letters came in an effort to turn that part of my life off and move on to the pencil-skirt-wearing woman I would be in three years. I had submitted my headshot to him months before but remembered the audition notice, because it sounded perfect for me: a talk show/skit-based daily show that revolved around our cultural obsession with weight and beauty.

Since my teen years spent showering at the gym, fitness had been a passion for me, and the gym a haven to hide out in when the world was too much to handle. But my time in LA, and the unfair expectations women were expected to live up to, had disgusted me. This was a show about all of those things.

The director told me to prepare a five-minute stand-up routine about nude yoga, so I spent a week entertaining myself in the bathroom mirror.

At the audition, an intern greeted me and took me to an unfinished and unventilated studio, bare except for the camera and tripod set up in the middle of the room. When she told me I could start, I stated my name, agent, and phone number, and began a tirade on the possibilities for group waxing during naked yoga class, and the matchmaking opportunities. The intern didn't give me much to go on, but I knew I was good. And when it was all done, I walked home thinking about the lifelong dream I would be giving up if I went to law school.

I got an email from the intern a few days later saying they wanted me to come in for a callback and to prepare another five-minute stand-up routine. This time I'd be auditioning for the show's director.

"Hi, Kimberly, I'm Sebastian. We talked a few weeks ago. Listen, I loved your first tape," the director greeted me when I walked in the door.

When I asked him if he could tell me more about the show I was auditioning for, he explained that Condé Nast was producing a new blog network made up of three sites: Daily Bedpost, about sex and relationships and tied to *Glamour;* Product Fiend, a makeup site connected to *Allure;* and Elastic Waist, which would be under the *Self* umbrella. This show was for Elastic Waist.

"We've already got some great bloggers on board, but we want to add a multimedia dimension and have a daily Web show reflecting current weight-loss trends and gimmicks."

Sebastian then went on to ramble a bit about his lovely fiancée, his history as an animator, and the new production company he'd launched. There was an Emmy in the corner that he didn't mention and so I didn't either, but it was clear that whoever Sebastian was, he knew what he was doing.

I didn't have to go back into the unventilated room this time; I set up shop in the middle of the production office and did my stand-up in front of the editors, animators, and interns.

I really wanted this, far more than I'd wanted any role since I'd done *The Importance of Being Earnest.* This show was about being myself on camera. I'd never done that before.

The call came a few days later.

"Hey, Kim, it's Sebastian — we met earlier this week. Listen, we just heard back from Condé Nast and they loved your tape. You're our host."

I wanted to get up and run around my office screaming while simultaneously puking in joy.

"That's great," I said instead. "What are our next steps?"

"They're going to call you about contract stuff, and after that's sorted out, we'll have you come in to shoot a promo."

"Thanks, Sebastian. I'm really looking forward to this."

"It's going to be great. Talk soon," he said before hanging up.

I squirmed a bit in my cubicle before calling my mother.

"I don't get it, it's a TV show for a magazine?"

"No, it's a blog associated with a magazine. Mom, what do I do about law school?"

"Don't go to law school."

"What? But this show could get cancelled after the first episode."

"Kim, I didn't tell you this while you were applying, but honestly, I don't think you should go to law school. I'm probably the only Jewish mother in the history of Jewish mothers to say this, but you're not a lawyer — this is what you were meant to be doing."

I wanted to believe my mom, but I really liked the fantasy world I'd built around being a lawyer: long intellectual conversations, nice suits, and paid vacation days. In my head, it seemed far more enticing than waiting around hallways with a bunch of people that look vaguely alike, each one hoping that they'll be the lucky one to give up their social life for the next three months for little to no pay and half-full audiences.

"Can I talk to Dad?"

My father's response was what I would expect from him. "I kind of liked the idea of you being a lawyer, but what do I know? Your mother is probably right."

I had the feeling my dad was really looking forward to three years of law school, of discussions with me about court cases and legal theory.

I asked the school I was most seriously considering for a deferment. I would have another year to decide whether or not to be a lawyer. Except a year later, I was still waking up at 5 a.m. every day to write headlines for the show, do my makeup and hair, and head over to the studio, where I would perform skits or go out on location to dance with Richard Simmons in the middle of Penn Station or interview Jillian Michaels at a fitness expo.

The show was nominated for a Webby Award and had accrued a respectable following, enough that I was asked to expand my role on the website and start writing daily columns for

Elastic Waist in addition to my on-screen time. My job was to be myself, on camera and in writing, and every day revolved around sharing another piece of myself with the world. With each post I sent to my producer for editing, I expected an email back saying that I was all sorts of screwed up and no one would want to read the inner ramblings of my insecure mind. But people did, and the reader comments that rolled in were from people who knew exactly how I felt, they said, because they felt the same way about their bodies, their stretch marks, and their daily battles with perfectionism.

A regular correspondent on our show had taken a job with a local news station and asked if I'd work for her there. After that I was approached by a fitness website. I'd gone from balancing a nonpaying acting career and office work to freelancing full-time as a blogger and hosting my own show.

Every morning I woke up and told myself to be thankful, that this wouldn't last forever. Nothing was ever this good for this long.

Brooklyn

TWENTY-SIX

I SPENT MY FIRST Condé Nast paycheck on a cruise. My mother had always dreamed of "eating her way across the ocean." We'd had less than a handful of family vacations in my life, and I wrapped the gift certificate with a giant beach ball and gave it to them for their twenty-fifth wedding anniversary.

"It's too much," my mother said.

"Well, I can't get my money back, so you'll just have to go."

"Are you coming with us?"

"No, I've got too much going on with work. You'll have to have fun for me, too."

Every few weeks when I went home to visit, I would ask if they'd figured out where they were going to go yet, and every few weeks they told me they were still thinking about it. It was well after their twenty-sixth anniversary that they announced that their big trip would be up the coast of Canada.

"Canada?" I said. "Not somewhere more exotic?"

"Well, your dad doesn't really like hot weather, and I just care about the food, so that seemed like a good compromise," my mom said.

While they were away, my father sent me photos from his

phone: Dad cuddling with a giant taxidermied bear, he and my mom grinning at dinner, animals made out of towels waiting for them in their cabin. They looked happy, like they always did when they weren't home.

"Hi, honey, we're home," the voicemail from my mom said. "We had a great time. Thank you again. Call me when you get this and I'll tell you about our trip."

When I called home it was my dad who answered — my mom wasn't feeling well, he said. "Your mom was in a lot of pain during the trip. Something's wrong with her stomach."

I called over and over again in the days that followed until she finally answered the phone from the hospital.

She relayed being in so much pain that she couldn't walk, and that she'd woken up my father in the middle of the night to hold her because she thought she was dying. He finally convinced her to go to the ER, but neither of them had considered calling me.

"I'm fine, I just need to get my gall bladder out," she said.

"Do you want me to come home?"

"No, I'll be in and out in a day. You can come out this weekend to help me."

TWENTY-SEVEN

"**D**ADDY, I CAN'T TALK. I'll call you back during my
lunch break," I whispered into my phone.

"I just got a call from Dr. Abdallah, Kim. There were
complications with Mom's surgery."

My mother had called me that morning to reassure me that
the surgery was no big deal and to make sure I was still planning
to come out to the Island to spend the weekend with her, watching movies and ensuring that my father ate a vegetable or two.

"He said it was serious. She's lost a lot of blood. We should get
there immediately." The words ran together as if he was afraid
that if he didn't get it all out in one shot he wouldn't be able to
get it out at all.

"Is she going to die?" It was all I could think of to ask — I
needed some sort of cue to tell me how to react.

"I don't know, Kim. It's certainly possible." His confusion was
evident. I don't think it had occurred to him in the past seventeen years, since her spine surgeries, that she might die before
him.

The truth is that it hadn't occurred to me either. I had always
expected this call, but I expected it to be my mom telling me that

my dad's heart had finally called it quits after years of peanut butter cups and cheeseburgers.

"Call me when you need to be picked up from the train."

"No, you go to the hospital. I'll meet you there." I was already half-packed. "I love you, Daddy."

"Right back at you, kiddo." His voice faded off.

I was working in Midtown, a block south of Central Park, and stumbled out of the building to grab a cab to Penn Station. I couldn't think, couldn't keep my mind in the present — it was a montage of my nine-year-old self, standing or sitting or sleeping by my mom's side in her hospital room or stepping outside to cry. But I wasn't nine anymore, there were things that needed doing. I pulled myself out of my stupor and called my aunt Lee. There was a train leaving in seventeen minutes according to the train schedule I kept in my purse. I'd carried one with me since I left Long Island, never knowing when I might need to get home in a hurry.

"What's happened?" There was no confusion on my aunt's end. If I was calling her at work, something was wrong.

Faced with relaying it all again, I understood why my dad said it so fast; saying it aloud made it real. I told her what I knew and in the same breath that she needed to come to Penn Station immediately. I didn't want to give her a choice. While my mother was fierce and nurturing, my aunt was the exact opposite: reserved and standoffish. I didn't trust that she'd get the severity of the situation or even then that she'd bother to drop everything and come running. But I needed her there for my mother, so I just told her exactly what to do.

I dashed to the Ronkonkoma-bound train gate where I'd told Lee to meet me. I had taken the train hundreds of times over the course of my life at all times of day, but on that day Penn Station was more crowded than I'd ever seen it on a weekday. I looked for Lee's big red tuft of hair, but I couldn't find her. I started crying.

I've always had the uncanny ability to fall apart in the most embarrassing places possible, yet when it's perfectly acceptable to express emotions in public to remain completely stoic. At my grandfather's funeral, when I was six, I pretended to cry because the woman next to me kept handing me tissues. I had been seated apart from my family; my parents, grandmother, aunt, and my aunt's boyfriend all sat in the front row of the funeral home as the rabbi said the kaddish. There was no room for me with them, so I sat in a row farther back with my parents' friend June. I didn't want June to feel bad, so I took tissue after tissue to dab my dry eyes. Later, when I told my mom, she said, "You take after my family; we hate letting anyone see us cry." In that moment, I had been so proud of that — my mom could handle anything, and I wanted to be just like her. I wondered how she'd feel about me now, beet-red and hyperventilating for all the station to see.

I stood alone in the whirl of commuters, who all avoided eye contact and kept their distance — all except one, a twentysomething man. He told the person he was on the phone with that he'd call them right back and came over to see if I was okay. "I'm okay, thank you." I said, forcing a smile and thinking about how nice people can be.

With three minutes left to boarding, there was still no sign of Lee, and I started making my way to the train. I wasn't about to miss it because she was too pigheaded to hustle. Which is, of course, when she finally showed up. I don't know that I could have forgiven her if she hadn't started running down the escalator. I pointed to the track and start running myself.

I didn't understand the bonds that siblings had, but I knew they were complicated. There was no one in my mother's life that could wound her with a flippant remark like my aunt, no one that she was harder on, and yet no one she defended as much. They didn't talk for five years after our house burned down — among other things, Lee had told our extended family that my mother burned down the house for the insurance money. They started talking again when my grandmother died, picking up right where they had left off.

The train was packed, and Lee and I found seats, thankfully secluded, by the conductor's box. Twenty minutes passed without a word, each of us staring out the window or at the floor. And then Lee started babbling on about her vacation to North Carolina. I wasn't expecting a hug or soothing words from her, but I didn't care for the distraction. My mother had earned the right to be the center of attention. I refused to make idle chitchat and instead brought the conversation back to what was slowly sinking in as my reality. "If she dies, I have to move home. I have to take care of Dad."

I couldn't help but think that if my mother died, my life was over, too. At that moment I wasn't sure if I wanted her to live more because I loved her or because if she was gone, so was my independence. I imagined my father's life without my mother: bills lost in piles of paper, mounds of laundry taking over as he continued to buy new clothes instead of washing old ones, dishes piled up in the sink until they were beyond cleaning, empty jars of Marshmallow Fluff and peanut butter littering the kitchen. My dad was so bad at adult things. He needed her. And without her, he'd need me.

"Your father can take care of himself," Lee said. Even she didn't believe it.

I started sobbing again and didn't stop for the rest of the hour-long ride.

Anna was waiting for us at the train station. She didn't say anything; she simply drove to the hospital, one hand on the steering wheel, one hand on mine. We saw Rachel, crying hysterically, as soon as we entered the hospital. I thought my mom was dead. "I can't lose my mom" was the only thing I could think of to say to her.

"I know," she said. "I just got here. They told me to find the surgical waiting room. Your dad is there."

I needed to get myself together before my mom saw me, before my dad saw me. I repeated orders in my mind: *Stop crying. Just breathe. Walk.* I just needed to get to the waiting room.

The room was empty except for my father and his newspaper. I had been to this hospital so many times over the years — asthma attacks, broken bones, blood drives — and there was an odd comfort in its familiarity. The waiting room had been renovated since the last time I was there. They had flat-screen TVs now, and blue carpet replaced the linoleum floors. It looked downright homey.

At first glance, my father could have been waiting anywhere for anything, just passing the time reading the news, but on closer inspection he wasn't reading the newspaper — he was touching it. Running his fingers through the pages, touching the corners, feeling around the headlines, the paper soothing him.

"Any news?" I honestly didn't know if I was ready to hear whatever he had to tell me. He'd never been the kind of parent to wipe away tears and whisper comforting words. We always had an unspoken agreement that he'd give me it to me straight, and in asking a question, it was my responsibility to determine if I really wanted to hear the truth.

"The nurse came in a few minutes ago." He lifted his head from his paper. "He said we could see her in recovery for a couple of minutes before they take her to the ICU." He was addressing everyone, but he only really seemed to be looking at me: scanning for damage, the way he did when I was a kid and would come home bruised and bloody from a run-in with cement.

The nurse returned to escort us to the post-surgical recovery area, where my mom was lying in a bed, eyes closed. It had been hours since I left the city, and I couldn't imagine what they'd been doing to her all this time. The nurse told us that she was sedated and couldn't hear anything we said, but there was a tear running down her face. I wondered if she knew what had happened. My dad spent a long time talking to her, and I was surprised he had that much to say. He wasn't exactly a demonstrative guy. When he stood up, I noticed the water in his eyes. It was the closest to crying I've ever seen him. My aunt passed on the opportunity to say anything to my mom, and so it was my turn.

"I need you. You can't leave me, okay? You can't leave me." I could have sworn that for a second she squeezed my hand. I didn't want to tell her I loved her or anything else that could be construed as a good-bye. She did not have my permission to die.

We waited for the doctor in the ICU waiting room. My father sat quietly, staring at his left hand. It was most likely a nervous habit, but I couldn't help but think he was looking for a wedding ring, something that would tie him to his wife.

My parents had never worn wedding rings. I bought them a pair for their sixteenth anniversary with the money I'd saved from my first waitressing job. I had their wedding date inscribed on the inside of the bands. They lost them days later. Things were always getting lost in our house — it was never worth the trouble of looking for them for fear of what else we might find.

TWENTY-EIGHT

DR. ABDALLAH ENTERED the waiting room. "You're all Mrs. Miller's family?" he asked.

"My kids and my sister-in-law," my father said. Rachel and Anna weren't blood, but they were practically my sisters. He must have known I'd need them there, and lied accordingly. It was a day of firsts; I'd never heard him lie before.

The ICU waiting room was tiny, which I only noticed once the five of us were forced to hold court uncomfortably close to the doctor. I'd read up on him before the surgery — I knew that he'd gone to medical school at the University of Baghdad, which community hospitals he was affiliated with, and that he had an average waiting-room wait time of twenty-five minutes — but I didn't realize how small he'd be. He was roughly my size, five foot four. He appeared to be about my parents' age, perhaps a few years younger.

I knew that he'd never say he was sorry for what had happened. He couldn't, legally, I was sure, but I could see it on his face, in his downcast eyes, as he told us what had happened in the operating room.

Complications. Lacerate. Liver. Kidney failure. Bile ducts. Laparoscopic. Bleeding. Sepsis.

I repeated the words over and over in my mind as he said them. I needed to remember all the details for my mom, so she could know what happened to her, and so I could try to figure out how to get her fixed. The surgery, Dr. Abdallah explained, took a turn for the worse when he accidentally severed the vein going to her liver. Since the surgery was laparoscopic, using small incisions for minimum invasion, they couldn't find the source of the bleeding quickly enough to prevent massive blood loss. In searching for the vein, they had ended up destroying her bile ducts. The lack of blood had caused her kidneys to go into distress.

"Is she going to die?" Apparently this was the only question I was capable of asking anyone, first my father and then the doctor. It's the only thing I cared about.

"She's not out of the woods yet. We'll know more in the next forty-eight hours." Dr. Abdallah looked as rattled as we did. He did these types of surgeries all the time. They weren't supposed to end like this. "The ICU nurses are helping to settle her. They'll come get you when you can see her."

"Thank you, doctor," my father said, as Dr. Abdallah turned to leave. He nodded and continued walking.

My father had always had a somewhat Norman Rockwellian view of doctors — and he was ready, willing, and able to chalk the whole thing up as an accident. I wasn't so sure. I saw Dr. Abdallah as careless — someone who, despite the abnormalities of her physique, assured my mother that everything would be A-OK. The part of me that wanted to protect my mother from everyone, including my father, wanted to throttle my dad for his "thank you." But the part of me that needed comfort curled up into him instead.

There was no one else that could have given me the all-encompassing bear hug I needed right then. My dad was the perfect size, his shoulder the perfect height. When I was a kid, he was trim and muscular, with curly blond hair and a bushy red beard. He'd filled out since then, his hair and beard turning a snowy white and his belly resting over the waistband of his jeans. In his flannel shirt and Long Island Ducks cap, he looked like a bus-driving Santa Claus.

No one else knew what to do. Rachel and Anna remained quiet, and Lee started babbling about how hard it was when my grandmother died, how losing her mother was something she was still coming to terms with. My dad stiffened at her words but said nothing. My grandmother was an old woman who died from old age. I still needed my mom. I needed her to say the right things when my heart was broken, to help me pick a wedding dress one day, to teach me how to be a mom. I was just starting my life, and she needed to be there for it. I could tell my dad was thinking along the same lines. "It's different," he whispered, and I burrowed myself deeper into his chest.

I knew what my mother would've said if she were there: that Lee was doing the best she could, that everyone has limitations to what they can give of themselves. She gave me this speech whenever I was angry with my father.

A nurse in purple scrubs entered the ICU waiting room and waved for us to follow her. "She's conscious, that's a good sign," she said.

The ICU was a big white and blue room with curtains separating the hospital's most critical patients. In the time since leaving the surgical recovery room, the nursing staff had hooked my mother up to more tubes and wires than I could count, all of them connected to machines that beeped sharply. My stomach lurched with each noise. When my mom saw us, she immediately started pointing to her breathing tube. She wanted it out, but we told her we couldn't. I wanted her to ask me for something I could give. I needed to feel like there was something I could do.

Once she realized we weren't going to pull the tube out, she changed tactics and signed for a pen. If there was one thing my dad was good for, it's a pen and paper. But her handwriting was shaky from anesthesia and all that came out was gibberish. She abandoned the written word in favor of using her finger to draw letters for us, as we stood around her bed shouting guesses in a game of charades.

She wanted to know what had happened to her and if she was going to die. I didn't want to tell her. I wanted her to think it was all totally normal. But I also wanted to be the one to deliver the news to her. I didn't trust anyone else to keep it gentle.

"The doctor nicked a vein, and because of the nature of the surgery, you lost a lot of blood. So in the next few days they're just going to monitor your internal organs to make sure everything goes back to normal," I told her.

In typical Mom fashion, she looked at me, looked at everyone else, then gave me a look of *yeah, right.* But no one countered my watered-down story.

The games continued. She pointed to her ears, making some sort of stabbing motion. She repeated it over and over. We were all confused, and she was angry with us — angry for not understanding her, angry for not taking the tube out so she could just tell us what she meant. I found myself getting defensive, the way I would when she'd call me out on my dating life or failed diets. She may have been dying, but she was still my mother.

I negotiated with God in my head: *If you let her live, I'll never get mad at her again.* Even though I knew this was an impossible promise — my mother could be absolutely infuriating — I added in a *I'll do something good with my life, something that will help people* for good measure. That was a promise I might actually be able to keep.

It was Lee who finally understood what she was trying to mime and spell out for us: My mother wasn't completely unconscious during the surgery.

She remembered hearing the ruckus in the operating room. She wanted to know what was wrong with her liver. She heard someone there say "mistake." She wrote the word "mistake" in the air with her fingers to emphasize that this was a direct quote. And then she spelled out Stony Brook. She wanted to be transferred to the hospital where I was born.

The nurse told us we needed to leave, that we were getting my mom too worked up. I asked her if it would be all right if I slept there.

"It's not allowed," she told me. "But I'm your mother's overnight nurse. If you just happen to wander in during the night, I won't mind. And a tip — the chairs in the waiting room convert into cots."

Anna offered to take Lee to the train, promising to come back tomorrow on her lunch break. I told my dad to go home and get some sleep. I had a feeling that he'd need to process this alone. Rachel helped me turn the chairs into cots and we settled in for the night. We'd been spending nights together in the hospital since we were born.

I knew that despite her vehemence in the ICU, my mother was fragile. If she were going to get through this, it would be because of me. I thought about all the times she told me the story of my premature birth, how she and my father were always there because they wanted me to know that I was loved and had people to live for. I knew that there was still a part of my mother that would try to take care of me, even now, a part that would protect me from having to watch her die. She'd spent years telling off mean teachers, school bullies, and the inner voice in my head that reminded me regularly that I was nothing more than the garbage I grew up in. I would protect her this time. I would promise her she was going to get out, as she had done for me so many times. And I would not leave her side, because if I did, I didn't trust her to keep fighting.

The week that followed blended together into one long day. I refused to leave the hospital, despite the pleas of my father and friends. I'd taken up residence in the waiting room, giving my credit card to Rachel and Anna so they could stop by Target and pick me up new clothes, shoes, clean underwear, toiletries, and reading material. I'd resorted to taking daily paper-towel baths in the handicap bathroom. The lone stall was the only place where I felt like I was really alone, and it became my place of refuge: a one-stop shop where I could bathe, cry, and pray that my mother would be allowed to live. It was the one place I could fall apart for a few minutes.

I was in the bathroom when she pulled out the catheter in her pulmonary artery. I'd only been gone a few minutes, but when I returned to her curtained-off corner of the ICU she was covered in blood and surrounded by nurses. She'd been asleep when she did it. Morphine had always given her nightmares, and she had been on a steady diet of it. Normally when she'd wake, I'd be there to take the brunt of her anxiety: In her medicated haze, she was always confused and angry. With each opening of her eyes, she'd demand that I leave her alone. I wasn't there to watch her that time, and instead of me, it was the wires she wanted gone. The nurses restabilized her and went on about their business. I planted myself in the chair by her bed and spent the next few days staring at her monitors.

The morphine and other drug cocktails kept her disoriented and frustrated. The doctors checked on her cognitive skills daily, and she answered mostly wrong. She couldn't remember my birthday or sometimes my name. She always gave my dad's information, my dad's birthday, my dad's name. He visited twice a day, before and after work, and each time he'd walk through the ICU door she'd whisper "Brian!" and reach for his hand and smile. When it was all falling apart, it was my father she reached out for. I had never seen this kind of affection between them. Perhaps this was the one good thing to have come from this, a reminder that my parents, despite their history of making one another miserable, loved each other.

When I wasn't allowed in the ICU, I spent my days swapping stories with other patients' loved ones, and when things were silent, I used my phone to look up information about the machines my mother was connected to. I looked for numbers that I should keep an eye out for, and when they appeared, I called the nurses. They didn't seem as concerned as I was. "If something's wrong an alarm goes off, and we'll come running. I promise," the nurse on shift assured me. I couldn't help thinking we needed to be more proactive than just waiting for an alarm to go off.

The first real inkling that the mom I knew was returning was when she called me over and whispered, "I don't always say what I mean. I want what I can't say I want." To most people this might have been drug-induced babble, but I spoke "Mom" pretty well. I knew that she was telling me she was going to fight them — it was a vital part of who she was. She needed to tell them not to touch her, or that she didn't want reparative surgery. "Listen to what people mean, not what they say" had been a mantra of hers, and she was telling me, in her way, what she meant. It was my job to make sure they did everything they could to save her.

True to her word, she fought them on everything, from linen changes to isotope scans. Legally, I was not her proxy — my father was — but the doctors and nurses looked to me to give the okay for her, and I did. The test results didn't do anything to lift our spirits. Her liver was not working. Her kidneys hadn't kicked in. But she was getting stronger despite her broken body, and almost two weeks after her surgery she was stable enough to be transferred to the ICU at Stony Brook.

Stony Brook University Hospital was the "good hospital," the hospital she should have gone to when her stomach pain started, but the ER at our tiny neighborhood hospital was less crowded. The Stony Brook ICU was a giant circle, and instead of curtains there were actual walls separating the patients. My mother had her own room, her own bathroom (not that she could use it), and a nurse that spent time with her and asked about her comfort levels.

Dr. Philipps, her new surgeon, was sweet and quiet. He was

tall and seemed uncomfortable in his own body, like a puppy with giant paws. There was a self-consciousness that came across in his mannerisms that was endearing. His arms folded and unfolded as if he wasn't quite sure what to do with them without some sort of medical instrument to act as a prop. Dr. Abdallah had spoken highly of him when he'd told me about the details of the transfer. "He specializes in gastrointestinal surgical oncology. He's very skilled in this area of the body. Your mother will be in good hands."

Dr. Philipps directed his questions to my mother, which I appreciated. She didn't know how to answer them, but I knew it mattered to her that he considered her the first source of information when it came to her own body. I filled him in on my notes from the other hospital, realizing how screwed up her medical records were. They said nothing about liver damage, but instead claimed that my mother was suffering from an infectious disease.

He appeared to believe me but couldn't necessarily take my word for it, and ordered a new batch of tests to determine the severity of my mother's injuries. For today, he said, "she should rest." Just being at Stony Brook made me feel like we had turned a corner. Her room was sunny, her doctor was thorough, and her nurses were much more proactive and attentive.

The words *strong* and *brave* had become interchangeable in my daily conversations with friends, family, and random hospital workers. *You're so strong. You don't have to be strong all the time. You need to be brave right now for your parents.* But I was not being particularly strong or brave. I was merely in a situation I had no other choice but to be present for. Mostly I was biding my time for my mother to be out of earshot so I could go back to crying.

Following another battery of tests, when Dr. Philipps made his rounds to my mother's room, he told us that our new plan was no plan. "Her body is too fragile. All we can do is watch her, monitor her kidney and liver functions, and hope the edema goes down."

She was moved from the ICU to the oncology floor, where most of Dr. Philipps' patients were. She didn't have cancer, but she needed the constant attention the nurses on that floor provided. It was a quiet floor with intermittent waiting rooms designed for families and the giving of bad news.

After two weeks, her kidneys started making urine again. Her liver was functioning, albeit on a slower scale, and there was nothing else Dr. Philipps could do for her right then. Her body was still too fragile to surgically repair the damages that Dr. Abdallah had created.

"There's no use in her staying here in the meantime. She should go home and be comfortable until we can do the surgery," Dr. Philipps said. I could tell that he thought that he was delivering good news.

"When do you think you'll release her?" I asked. I wanted him to say a week. Or two weeks. A month would have been great.

"A couple of days, probably by the end of week."

I thanked him. I circled the oncology floor trying to quiet my brain enough to come up with a plan. All I could think of was filth. She was going to leave the hospital, go back to the apartment, and be surrounded by filth. She was going to slip on papers or fall over broken computers, abandoned boxes, and the plethora of shoes that made their home in my parents' living room. She wasn't strong enough to stand on her own and there was no way she'd be able to navigate their home like that, no way her walker would fit through the piles. This was the first time that I'd ever really resented my father.

Before there was ever a word for hoarding, I knew that whatever driving force drew my father to garbage was beyond his control. I never felt like he loved stuff more than he loved me. He loved stuff. And he loved me. I never blamed him for that. But I would blame him if something happened to my mother.

Until then, the only act of rebellion I'd ever followed through on in my life was piercing my navel. My generally liberal parents believed that body piercings were disgusting. Luckily, I had friends who saw things my way. For my eighteenth birthday, Anna took me to the local tattoo parlor to get my belly button punctured. It was the winter break of our freshman year of college, and it was terrible timing. Piercings need to be cleaned regularly, and for the next three weeks I would be living in a house without running water. I took to cleaning it out in store bathrooms and friend's houses, but the infection that came was inevitable. My stomach still bears a keloid scar from the mass infection that took over my lower abdomen for the majority of 2001.

Eight years later, my mother was leaving the hospital with a hole in her abdomen. Instead of a ring, hers had a tube protruding from it with a grenade-shaped plastic ball hanging from the end, collecting the bile that her gallbladder was once responsible for. Over the previous few weeks, I had listened numerous times to her nurses as they explained how important it was to keep her wound clean, that the hole led directly into her stomach cavity and an infection could kill her.

In the years since leaving home, I had cleaned my parents'

apartment countless times. Each time I swore it would be the last. Each time they were embarrassed and grateful and promised it would never get that bad again. They never kept their promises, but even the clutter and filth of their current apartment was a reprieve from the abject squalor of my childhood home, and I was grateful for that. I hadn't purged their apartment in over six months, attempting the tough-love approach to parenting my parents while I went about my daily life, running between auditions, shoots, and blog deadlines. I had hoped that without me to fall back on, they'd see the error of their ways and clean their own apartment. I was tired of being asked to "help." I was tired of asking Anna and Rachel to take weekends off from their lives and families to help me manage mine. But my plan had backfired, because the apartment was at its messiest yet, and I needed to dig them out yet again.

Pacing the oncology ward, there was only one person I could think of to call, and it wasn't Anna or Rachel. Not my father, or my aunt, or my boss. It was my friend Abby, Paul's old friend from Brandeis.

In the years since my breakup with Paul, I had become close with several of his friends, especially Abby . . . she knew me as the woman I had become since leaving Long Island. I was a comedienne and a writer, and I had my life together. Abby grew up not far from me, on the East End of Long Island, where her mother owned a cleaning company that serviced well-to-do Hamptonians. We shared stories about our upbringings, and she'd often joke about her childhood wearing Armani and Burberry, the hand-me-downs of her mother's clients. I joked about my hippie-dippie parents and overachieving rebellion. I never talked about how I lived. Aziz, Becky, and Abby knew me as the person I'd always wanted to be, and now I was about tell her who I really was.

Abby had dropped by the hospital a few days earlier, on her way east to visit her own family. She brought magazines and flowers and reminded me that if I needed anything I should give her a call.

I don't think she realized what kind of call she was inviting me to make, and as the phone rang, I realized I should have probably practiced this speech a couple of times in my head beforehand.

"Hey, lady. How's your mom?"

"Hey, Abs. She's a fighter," I told her. "They're actually going to be releasing her from the hospital later this week. They can't do corrective surgery for a few months, not until the edema goes down."

"That's great — well, that she gets to go home."

"Actually, that's why I'm calling." I was exhausted and desperate, but more than anything I felt like I was about to sacrifice everything for clean carpets yet again. "I was wondering if your mom or any of her employees are looking for some extra work? I want to make sure my parents' house is clean enough for my mom."

"Oh, sure, I'll call her now. I'll be out on the Island this week. I can help."

"Abby, this isn't a small job. I'll be there cleaning, and I'm sure Anna and Rachel will help too." I didn't know how to say it all without saying it. "My dad's a hoarder."

A year or two prior, no one would have known what that meant, but thanks to A&E, people plagued with the compulsive need to collect were now the subject of cult fascination. I didn't find comfort in that fact. "The house is pretty bad. I usually come home to help every few months, but I haven't been on top of it. Please let your mom know I'll pay whatever it takes — it's a lot of work, I'll try to do most of it."

"Don't worry, hon, they've seen it all before. I'll talk to my mom and let you know what she says."

Based on Abby's reaction, it was clear to me that she didn't realize just how big of a mess it really was.

TWENTY-NINE

WHEN I CAME ACROSS the many shows about hoarders, I would promptly change the channel. I couldn't even stand to watch commercials for them. I imagined casting directors scouring piles of applications from those so desperate for help they would willingly exploit themselves and their families, for those they believed would have the most outrageous stash or spectacular nervous breakdown on the front yard. The people on shows like *Hoarders* weren't my parents, but there was a part of me that wanted to protect them as if they were. Because like my own parents, I was sure that they were more than their disease. Many of them were probably parents who rubbed achy bellies, told bedtime stories, and waited outside dance recitals with bouquets of roses.

I had spent my life protecting my family's secret, keeping it close to my heart and surrounding it with revisionist stories, and now that I'd told Abby, it was finally out in the world. I didn't know how to protect my parents from the judgment I knew was imminent. Abby and her mom would come to my aid; they would help clean out my parents' apartment, because I needed help and they were good people. But I wasn't sure what would happen after that. How could I explain that my parents really were the sweet, funny, loving people that they were — and yet they lived the way that they did?

I decided not to tell my mom yet about my confession to Abby. I wanted to tell my dad first and give him a say in the matter. It was his secret, after all, even if she was the one who was ashamed of it.

"These flowers have really lasted a long time!" my mom said when I wandered into her hospital room, alert for the first time in weeks. She didn't know it, but I'd been going to the hospital gift shop while she was asleep to buy new bouquets. Her room was full of flowers and cards and cute knickknacks I got her, racking up quite the credit card debt in the process. I told her they were from my dad and me. I just wanted to make her happy.

The fact that she noticed the longevity of the flowers around her was a good sign. In a moment of clarity or stubbornness, she demanded that her morphine intake be reduced drastically, afraid she might become addicted. The morphine-reduced version of her was more normal, which meant she was back to being angry with my dad instead of with me.

"Where is your father? He should have been home from work an hour ago!"

She then turned her sights to me. "Have you eaten?"

"Where is your father?" and "Have you eaten?" were the two most common sentences in my mother's lexicon.

My father was late for just about everything — he'd lose hours at a time and have no idea what he did with them. But I did. He would get lost rifling through one of his plastic bags or listening to NPR on one of his radios. I was sure that at that moment he was in the parking lot, rummaging through his car for a portable one to bring into the hospital so he wouldn't have to miss *Talk of the Nation.*

"Calm yourself, Mamala." I replied. "He came by on his lunch break to see you, but you were sleeping. He brought me a sandwich."

"And no one thought to wake me?" she retorted. "I'm glad I matter so much to him he can't even ask how I'm doing."

"I gave him a rundown of the day," I told her.

"That's nice, but you're not his wife."

I was relatively certain that I would not be able to keep my promise not to get angry at my mother, but this was a good sign — my mother, perpetually afraid that she wasn't loved enough, was on her way back to the living.

My father then walked into the room, carrying a portable radio connected to headphones — one earbud in, one earbud out — and wearing a large shopping bag like a purse.

My mother growled at him, baring her teeth.

He laughed, slapping his thigh. "Someone's feeling better, I see!" He waved a hello.

While she was in a drugged haze, my dad kissed her on the forehead when he came and left. But now that ended. My mom hated kissing, always had. Every once in a while, my mom would accidentally tell my dad she loved him, at the end of a phone call or as he left the house, a force of habit generally reserved for me. She'd blush, cover her mouth and ask, "Do you think he heard me?"

After a short while my mom nodded off, which she was prone to do every hour or so, and I told my dad about Abby.

"I'm going to have to do some cleaning before the crew gets there," I said. "It's too much to do in one day."

There was an immediate shift in his physique; his hands took up residence in his pockets and his broad shoulders rounded forward. My sixty-three-year-old father looked like a high school kid on the verge of suspension.

"Okay, what do you need me to do?" he asked.

When Rachel and Anna would help me clean my parents' apartment, we spent hours, sometimes days, throwing things out, but the house never truly got clean, just less messy. But what my mother needed now, with a hole in the middle of her body, was clean — which was why I needed professional help. Which was why I had to tell our secret to yet another friend.

"Dad, can you take a few days off work to stay with Mom while I clean?"

"I can do that."

"You can't screw it up this time. I need you to really try to keep it clean."

"I'll try," he said.

"I don't want this to come out the wrong way," Anna said. "I love your parents, but every time we do this, I get so mad at them. I just can't believe this is how you grew up."

But this was nothing compared to how I grew up. Anna never saw the inside of our old house, and it is probably best that she imagined it looking more like the new apartment than what it did when we fled from it eight years ago: like the damp and mucky remnant that collects at the bottom of Dumpsters. At least this place was dry dirty.

"Me too," I replied.

I had hoped we'd be farther along by now. Despite my confession to Abby, I thought that Anna and I could do the bulk of the work before she and the rest of the designated cleaning crew got here. I underestimated my own exhaustion level, and my parents' ability to fit large quantities into small spaces.

Anna held up a fifty-state commemorative quarter holder. It was empty. My dad had Ziploc bags of quarters hidden all around the apartment — many more collected than that cardboard memento could hold.

"Toss it," I said.

One of the few things my father had inherited from his own father was a collection of rare old coins. They, along with everything else we owned, burned up in our house, but for each holiday or birthday after the fire my mother would buy my father a new old coin, neatly preserved between layers of cardboard and plastic, to help rebuild his lost collection. I knew his coins were special, but that didn't stop me from stealing them anyway, to buy an orange New Kids on the Block lunch box when I was nine.

When he noticed he'd been robbed, he didn't yell at me. This happened shortly after he returned from the mental hospital, and I think he realized how close he was to losing his family. He never yelled at me again after the radio incident — instead, when I admitted that I had stolen his old coins to buy a four-dollar lunch box, he just shook his head.

At this point, he had come to expect the things he loved to be gone each time I come to visit. He still gives me bear hugs when he picks me up from the train and says "my baby girl" with his big growly laugh as his arms engulf me.

Cleaning has never been easy for me, and I have always been self-conscious about it, convinced that no matter how much dusting, mopping, and sweeping I do, I will never really be clean enough.

My junior year of college, I moved off-campus to a beautiful three-bedroom apartment on the outskirts of Boston with two friends. Unlike the lavish dorms I'd been living in, there was no cleaning staff to maintain our space; I had learned to be tidy, but I hadn't learned to clean, and I was petrified of being outed as hygienically impaired.

When no one was home, I studied the labels on cleaning bottles, made notes on how to use them, and did Internet searches on the regularity with which each chore should be performed. I cleaned in private, hoping no one would know that it was me who mopped the floor or scrubbed the toilet, afraid I would be accused of doing it wrong. Afterward I would blow-dry the mop so there was no evidence of its use.

I've gotten better over the years. I let my mops dry naturally now, and I've been able to keep my tiny Brooklyn apartment clean and orderly and normal. Seamus moved out shortly after I started hosting the show, and with my improved income, I opted to skip the Craigslist roommate search and keep the two-bedroom for myself. Despite my years of studying the labels of various cleaning products and learning proper scrubbing protocol via instructional YouTube videos, I still found comfort in hiring someone to deep-clean my apartment twice a month. Of course, I would sweep and Swiffer before she showed up, lest she judge me as slovenly.

My parents' home is something else entirely. The papers are the easy part, but once they're bagged and off to the dump, next comes the stuff. They have so much stuff. My father loves electronics, the more broken and useless the better. And office supplies. Bundles of Post-it notes, pens, pencils, scientific calculators, hole punchers, and staplers can be found in every room. While my mother's postsurgical depression has certainly lessened over the years, her compulsive shopping for things they do not need with money they do not have did not. She will never admit that she is part of the problem now, insisting that she will return most of what she buys. But things don't get sent back; they have a habit of being engulfed by the stuff surrounding them. Each new box added to the house becomes a new surface to put things on.

There was a brief moment in time, when I was eleven or twelve, when my parents had hired cleaning people to come in once a month. We never had the money or nerve to allow them the time to clean the whole place out, but my mother had moments of lucidity from her depression when she could see how bad the house was getting. A team of workers would come in with face masks and shovels to rid us of garbage. In a day, they could usually succeed in digging us out of one room. But that was all we could afford, and by the next time we were able to pay them to come back, that room would be full again, and they would need to start all over.

For what little time we had it, I loved that one clean room. If we could just keep it clean for a whole month, then the following month the cleaning people could get to a different room, then another one, and maybe in a year we could have a clean house again. Another fresh start.

We've continued the pattern over the years, only my parents no longer bother to have a cleaning crew come in. They know

I will clean their house, and I know I will be back to start from scratch in a matter of months.

Abby's mom arrived with one of her most zealous employees in tow. Reina was shy and sweet, and smiled at me and at my parents' dump of an apartment like she'd just entered the gates of Disney World. Abby's mother, rail-thin and strong as an ox, asked me what I'd like Reina to start working on first. I looked around at the overwhelming task we all had in front of us.

Anna and I have been cleaning for two days, and the apartment still looks like hoarder central.

"Why doesn't she start with the bathroom, okay?" Abby's mom said. I stayed silent, wallowing in guilt — I should be able to take care of my family on my own, but I'd been too pigheaded to come home over the last few months to help my parents.

My excuses included dates, work, and shooting schedules, but the truth was I was just tired of cleaning up after my parents. I refused to accept that this was just who my parents were, and still stubbornly thought that if I let them stir in their own stuff long enough, they might change.

"Wow" was all Abby's mom said as she walked around the apartment, surveying the damage.

"It's just really hard for my dad; he doesn't see how much there is, and my mom can't clean — it's hard for her physically."

I was exhausted and embarrassed, and I wanted to make excuses for my parents like I always had. It was easiest to blame it all on my father. He so willingly accepted the blame, and my mother had just escaped death, which meant she got a get-out-of-blame-free card for the moment.

"It's okay. I'm not going to throw anything out. I'm going to move it, and whether to get rid of it will be your decision or your parents'. My job is to clean around it. It'll be okay."

Over the course of the day, I excused myself more often than was fair to take bag after bag to the development compactor, leaving Anna, Abby's mother, and Reina to do most of the heavy lifting for me. But I needed to be away — to remember why I was doing this. I was cleaning for my mother, because I loved her, because I wanted her to be safe. I needed to remind myself of that, because cleaning my parents' home, more than anything else, made me angry.

I hadn't thought about my childhood in years. Even when I went back to clean my parents' apartment, I could avoid thinking about my childhood home. I remembered the basics, but the images were gone. The reality of my parents had never been escapable, but somewhere along the way of life I forgot how truly bad it was, and intermittently forgot to be ashamed.

When I got back from the compactor, my friend Becky was on her hands and knees, scrubbing my parents' kitchen floor with a cleaning brush. Abby had called her, and she'd driven in from New Jersey to help with the cleaning efforts. A few minutes later, Abby arrived, bottles of soda in hand. Rachel and Tim would arrive later in the day. I was both thankful and nervous for the day to end, because when it was all over, I knew there would be questions. Abby and Becky would ask me why I never told them, or worse, they wouldn't ask. They could just as easily forget to invite me to Rosa Mexicano's for pomegranate margaritas after work, then to birthdays, then to their upcoming weddings, and eventually I would be someone they used to know, that girl who seemed so normal.

THIRTY

WHEN THE DAY WAS OVER, every inch of my parents' apartment had been scoured. When things were clean enough, they were cleaned again, and once they were cleaned again they were organized. The pantry had been emptied of expired goods; the piled-up clothes in my parents' closets had been rehung on the fancy hangers my mother had ordered at one point but never used. Cobwebs were removed and colonies of insects were vacuumed out from under and inside furniture. I had gotten new table linens and shoe holders and a variety of storage boxes to help keep things contained. It looked like clean people lived there. It looked like a place safe enough for my mom to live in.

I had cleaned out my savings account to pay for the deep clean, but no one accepted my money. Not my friends, not Abby's mother, not even Reina, the woman they hired to come help us.

"This is how life works," Abby's mom said. "When we need help, you can come clean for us."

I should have felt like a charity case, another shame to add to those caused by my filthy house and crazy family and especially regarding Reina, who was paid by Abby and her mother. But I was just too utterly exhausted to feel anything but gratitude.

My father would do what he was told, methodically and faithfully, but I knew he wouldn't intuit what my mother needed. Especially if she was too proud to ask, which would often be the case. She needed help standing, she needed to be forced to eat, and her bedsores and surgical wounds needed tending. I had waking nightmares of my mom taking her anger and frustration out on my dad and him doing what he had always done when under attack — walking away and leaving her there. Their house was clean, but I still couldn't let her go home. After her release from the hospital, she came home with me.

Like my parents and grandparents, I had a room in my apartment that I didn't use — Seamus' old room. Unlike my parents and grandparents, it was completely empty, except for a desk. I fancied this room my office, but mostly just used it for exercise and as a guest room when friends visited. I set my mother up there after unsuccessfully trying to give her my bedroom.

"It's the air mattress, or I go home with your father," she said. "I'd rather sleep on the plastic; it's easier to clean up." She was petrified that the plastic grenade–shaped ball filled with the brown fluid that drained from her abdomen would leak and ruin my mattress.

Allowing my mother to sleep on an air mattress seemed cruel, but it turned out she was right. When I woke up the next morning, my dad was standing over my bathroom sink hand-washing my sheets.

"Hey, kiddo, Mom and I had an adventure. Those grenade thingies should really have a screw top."

I found my mother in the guest room, sitting on the naked air mattress, sobbing.

"It's okay, Mamala. It's really no big deal."

"It is a big deal. What have I become?"

After almost a month in a hospital bed, she had wasted away. Her waist-length red hair started to come out by the fistful. She was afraid to brush it, afraid of pulling out more, so her loose hair had tangled itself into a knob at the base of her head. Her underwear fell off her when she stood, and she needed help getting off the couch and toilet.

My mom, who, once upon a time, never cried, now cried all the time. She cried on the couch watching television. She cried when I needed to lift her off the toilet. And she cried in the shower, because I had to hold on to her so she wouldn't fall.

"I'm so sorry, Kimmy. You shouldn't have to do this."

"Mama, there's really no one else in the world I'd like to hang out in the shower with." I tried at levity.

"Oh boy, do you need a boyfriend."

After two weeks of recuperating at my house, my mother was getting stronger, crying less, and becoming more independent with the help of her walker. She wanted to go home and return to some semblance of her own life. And as worried as I was, I was also excited by the prospect of some solitude.

I called my dad to arrange her homecoming, but also to check on the status of their apartment; it'd been two weeks since my friends came and purged it of all signs of my parents' true nature, and I was afraid that he had filled the whole place up again.

"Hey, kiddo, how's Mom?" He sounded like he was having far too much fun living alone.

"Good. She wants to come home. I think she's officially sick of me. How's the apartment holding up?"

"It's good."

"How good?"

"Good good."

"Does it look like it looked when I left it?"

"Pretty much."

"'Pretty much' does not instill confidence."

"Kim, it's good, really. There are some newspapers on the table, but not a lot. I haven't screwed it up."

"Sorry, Daddy."

"It's okay. How did I raise such a neat freak?"

He really did see it that way—that he just had some stuff laying around and I was a pedantic minimalist. When I would explain to him that he was, in fact, a hoarder, he would accept it, but he'd also accept being a Smurf if I insisted he was one.

"Just lucky I guess," I responded. "So, wanna come collect your wife on Saturday?"

"Do I have to?" he said, laughing.

"I'm going to tell her you said that . . ."

"Oh no!" He laughed again, more heartily. "I'll be there bright and early Saturday."

After she went home, I spent most of my downtime out on Long Island with them, helping around the house, going to doctors' appointments with her, and attempting to keep my father from bringing new garbage into the house.

Three months later, in late January, my mom was stable enough to go into corrective surgery. She had been stable enough in December, but she didn't want to ruin our holidays if something went wrong again.

We were barely inside the triage room before we were greeted by a very excited med student.

"It's great to meet you, Mrs. Miller," he said as he shook my mother's hand. "This is a big case." He went on to babble excitedly about how he got to the hospital early so he would be first in line to scrub in.

"I'm sure Dr. Philipps has taught you well, and I'm glad to be in such competent hands," my mother says. "I look forward to thanking you in person after the surgery."

After he left, she turned to me. "I'd rather he liked me before he starts tinkering around inside me with a scalpel."

A parade of doctors and nurses came in to introduce themselves and test my mother's vital signs, and the reality that we were doing this again sank in. It was starting to seem like the only way I knew my mother was either going into surgery or recovering from it. Meanwhile, my father was sleeping on a round rolling chair — no small task, given its propensity to roll off and wake him up. Each time he was jarred into semiconsciousness, I shot him a dirty look. My mother could die, and he would have spent his last few moments with her snoring on a stool.

"Let him sleep," my mom said.

"I can't believe him."

"This is how he copes with stress, he checks out."

"When did you become the patient one in the family?"

"I'd rather have him sleeping here than roaming the halls of the hospital stealing brochures about diabetes and prenatal care."

We kissed my mother good-bye and set off to take our rightful places in a corner alcove of the surgical waiting room. We had spent so much time in this hospital over the preceding few months that it had started to feel like a second home.

My father could pass hours upon hours of waiting immersed in books about finances and magazines about computer software. I couldn't. Allowing anything but my mother to take up space in my mind felt like a betrayal.

"Remember when Mom made you wear a suit to my fifth grade field trip to Philadelphia?" It had been almost 100 degrees that day, but she hadn't wanted me to be embarrassed by my father's usual uniform of too-loose jeans and faded T-shirts with chest pockets bursting with business cards and scrap paper.

My father laughed as if he were remembering the best day of his life. "Yeah, your mom's a pisser. Next time I'll know better."

"And the time you had pneumonia?" My mother woke up in the middle of the night to check his fever and had found him burning up. She ran to the bed with ice packs to place all over him to bring the fever down — but she forgot to wake him up first. His screams woke the next-door neighbors up.

My father laughed so hard that the people around us, other people waiting to know the fate of loved ones in surgery, sent glares our way.

"Daddy, what if she dies?"

My father stopped laughing and put his hand on my knee. "I don't know if this makes any sense to you, but I've asked the universe to watch out for Mom, and I think it's going to be okay."

My father prayed. He never stopped surprising me.

THIRTY-ONE

THIRTEEN HOURS OF SURGERY and another month of hospital living later, we were finally free to resume some semblance of our normal lives again. My mother had her own battles to fight: frailness far beyond her years and a body made patchwork by surgical scars, in addition to her ever more faltering eyesight. I wanted to go home and be with her again, to pull her out of a depression I knew was imminent, but I couldn't. I could hardly look at her or my father.

After the mass cleanout of their apartment, I had been plagued by nightmares. Nightmares about my old house: images of sludge-filled puddles in the kitchen, fly droppings that covered every window, and maggots in our food. I dreamed about sucking my stomach in so that I could squeeze through the front door despite the trash pushing it closed, the sounds that emanated from the attic, and the stranger who lived alongside of us.

I dreamed about the decision I had made to use a broken toilet, knowing full well that my feces would live in it indefinitely, rather than soil myself, because I didn't know the next time I would have a proper shower.

I dreamed about fleas. It had been almost ten years since I'd seen a flea or even thought about their existence, but I woke up sweating and scratching the little red bumps that took over my body while I slept.

These were all parts of my life that I had put away.

For months I woke up between 1 a.m. and 3 a.m., sweat-drenched and scratching. The nightmares had expanded from fleas, and I started remembering floors covered in animal feces, ceilings crumbling as they rotted, and our swimming pool — the pool we used one summer but then never closed and allowed to become a brown pond filled with waste. We went out of town one weekend only to find that a neighbor climbed over our fence and threw our dog in the pool. He had been swimming in the brown water for hours, we think, when my father jumped in to get him. When my father came out he was covered in a thick greenish brown sludge.

When I woke up, I cleaned. Every night I wiped down my floors with bleach and sprayed bug spray on my bed. It smelled noxious, yet comforting.

Every subway car in New York City was plastered with ads for bedbug remedies: mattress covers that claimed to contain bugs and dogs that could sniff out insects that humans couldn't find. I convinced myself that those tiny bloodsucking miscreants were the reason for my incessant itching.

By April I was so sleep-deprived and so convinced that it was bugs causing my nightmares that I woke up my landlord in the middle of the night, banging on his door and telling him that he needed to hire an exterminator immediately.

"Okay, Kimberly," my landlord, John, said. "I'll call an exterminator. Can it wait until morning?"

When I returned to my apartment, I threw out my blankets, pillows, and sheets — anything I thought bugs could hide in. I threw out boxes of mementos, the bag that held my once-beloved dance shoes and leotards, picture frames and books, my alarm clock and my nightstands — and then I dismembered my bed.

I grabbed a 10-inch chef's knife from my kitchen and used it to slice open the box spring, then climbed inside, flashlight blazing, to inspect each crevice of the thin, paperlike material on the bottom and the wood frame for signs of a bug infestation.

I didn't see any, but based on my nightly Internet bedbug research, I knew that didn't mean anything. Just because you couldn't see them didn't mean they weren't there.

I mopped with bleach again and sprayed another layer of bug spray on my stripped bed, then blew up my air mattress to sleep on.

The next morning, I called to see if my doctor could fit me in.

"Those aren't bedbug bites; those are hives," he said, inspecting the bumps on my arms, legs, stomach, and back.

"Are you sure? I wake up scratching in the middle of the night every night." I neglected to tell him about the nightmares, about my old house and the fleas.

"Yes, I've seen a lot of bedbug bites in the last few years. Hives can be caused from an allergy or from stress. Have you changed detergents or been particularly stressed lately?"

I told him about my mother, but that she was doing better.

"I shouldn't be stressed anymore."

He wrote me a prescription for antihistamines that would both stop my itching and put me to sleep.

I was furious — I couldn't believe my doctor had been so incompetent — and raced home to meet the exterminator. I presented him with evidence of my infestation: particles of dust (or dead bug bodies) that I had found in my home and carefully preserved in Ziploc bags for safekeeping. He assured me that I didn't have bedbugs.

"Listen, I could charge you a lot of money to fumigate this place, but you don't have bedbugs," he reported to me in a thick Brooklyn accent.

"Thank you," I said.

When he left my apartment, I called Rachel.

"What happened? Is your mom okay?" she asked as she answered the phone. I told her about the nightmares and the bedbugs.

"Kim, I'm worried about you," she said. "This is what you do whenever you're upset — you throw out your stuff. But since you don't have much stuff to throw out, you've created some sort of physical manifestation for your PTSD."

"I don't have PTSD, I'm just really itchy."

That night I woke up at 3 a.m., sweating and itchy despite my antihistamine, and resigned myself to the fact that I didn't have bedbugs. I just hadn't dealt with my childhood.

THIRTY-TWO

As I RELAYED THE STORIES — CPS scares, the house burning down, my grandmother kicking us out, the new house, my father's brain injury and his time in the mental hospital, my suicide attempt, and my mother's inability to have a surgery that didn't almost kill her — I imagined the therapist sitting across from me was writing PATHOLOGICAL LIAR in big bold letters in her notepad, then circling it over and over and over again. The abbreviated version of my life didn't sound real, even to me.

"Honestly, I don't think you're depressed, at least not chemically," she said as I rummaged through my purse to find money to pay her. "I don't think you need medication. I think you've gone through a lot, and you need to find peace with it."

I didn't know what "finding peace" meant. Forgive my parents? No need, there was nothing to forgive; they'd done the best they could. Their best was slightly less best than some other people's, but not as bad as child molesters or belt-yielding abusers. They were unfathomably messy, not evil. I still loved my parents, probably more obsessively than anyone else I knew loved theirs, so I didn't really see how this therapy thing was going to help me. I just wanted a pill that would make my nightmares go away.

I didn't tell the therapist all this, though. When she asked if I'd like to see her again, I agreed to her suggestion of once a week.

Hoarders was on TV for two years before I could bring myself to watch it, but in the months following my first therapy session I made learning everything I could about hoarding a pet project — one that would hopefully help me "find peace." Whatever that meant. On a rainy Saturday, with nothing better to do, I sat down for a Netflix-fueled *Hoarders* binge. I wanted to see what the world saw when they were exposed to hoarding.

The houses with children were the ones that broke me down. I remembered what it felt like to look at a parent who loves you and to be ashamed of them, and be ashamed that you are ashamed. When a house on the show was "clean" — when people collected things in themes and could still see their floors and their food wasn't rotten and their toilets still worked and they could shower at home — I had a sort of indignant pride. *That's nothing compared to how I grew up!*

Episode after episode, I cried — not because of what was on TV, but because I knew that there were people, millions of people, who watched shows like this for fun. People who laughed and feigned gagging, people who would never really understand what it felt like to live like that.

A twenty-one-year-old man, a hoarder living with an alcoholic father, made my stomach turn inside out. *How often does this happen?* I thought, then pressed pause.

I immediately started searching for a tie between alcoholic parents and hoarding children and stumbled upon the website for the National Association for the Children of Alcoholics. On a page titled "Effects of Alcoholism on the Entire Family," it stated that children of alcoholics are four times more likely than the general population to become hoarders.

I called my parents.

My mom answered. "Hi, honey, we're watching *The Tourist.*"

"I can call back later."

"No, that's okay, we paused it. What's up?"

"I was just doing some research and I stumbled upon a site that said that children of alcoholics have a higher incidence of hoarding than those born to nondrinking parents."

"That sounds about right," she said. My mother had always told me that she thought my father behaved like a "dry drunk," interacting with the world as if an addict, not because he was one, but because he had been raised by them.

"I just wanted to call and . . ."

" . . . give Dad an excuse."

"I guess so."

"Okay, here, talk to your dad."

"Hey hey, K-Rae!" I heard my father's voice beam out, and I realized that my parents were having a nice day and I was calling to ruin it.

"Hey, Daddy, I just wanted to call and report my latest find."

When I started doing research into hoarding after my first therapy session, I decided that I would share what I found with my dad. I wanted to understand, and I wanted him to understand why he was the way he was. And there was no one I knew who appreciated knowledge — any form of information, really — as much as he did.

Over the years I had learned not to give my parents things as gifts, but I broke my own rule and bought my father a copy of *Stuff: Compulsive Hoarding and the Meaning of Things,* a book that featured profiles of various types of hoarders.

He found the book fascinating, even flattering at points, when the book's authors, professors Randy Frost and Gail Steketee, theorized that hoarders may actually be smarter than the rest of us, able to see connections in things that others can't.

But most important, the research opened up an avenue of discussion for us.

"Okay," he said. "How am I crazy today?"

I relayed the new finding about alcoholic parents. He said, "Does that make me *eight* times as likely because both of my parents were drunks?"

"If there's one thing I've learned from therapy: You can blame everything in your life on your parents," I told him. "I just wanted to give you a little fodder."

"Oh well, then, thank you."

In my reading I found that many hoarders have similar stories to my dad. Maybe they weren't the children of abusive alcoholics, but they were emotionally neglected at some point in their development. One of the more popular theories behind the triggers for hoarding indicates that people who were neglected emotionally as children learn to form attachments to objects instead of people. When they do connect with others, they then keep any object that reminds them of that person as a way of holding on to those attachments.

Every visit home comes with a stack of newspaper clippings my father has saved for me, fitness magazines he thinks I will be interested in, or notes on software he thinks I would find helpful. I usually just throw them out.

-

THIRTY-THREE

"I WOULDN'T MIND A PLACE like this," my dad said, putting his arm around my shoulder.

My extended family invited my parents and me to seders and Thanksgivings every five years or so out of obligation, but an invitation to just come by and visit was a rarity that I couldn't remember ever happening. But when my mother was in the hospital, her cousin Sue started calling regularly, and when my mother healed enough to get around again without her walker, Sue invited the lot of us to Pennsylvania for a visit.

Sue's house was practically made of windows, without blinds drawn or dark impermeable curtains. My parents had never opened a single curtain to let in natural light, always afraid of who might see in.

"You can have something like this, Dad," I replied.

He nodded and tightened his grip around my shoulder.

"So," Sue said to my aunt Lee and my mother, "which one of you is a hoarder like your parents?"

My mother made eye contact with me and then pointed a

sheepish finger in my father's general direction. I had no idea what was going on.

"My parents never threw anything out," my mother later confessed on the train ride back. "They had someone in regularly to clean, but there was always stuff everywhere. I remember thinking how great it was that they had a room reserved for junk."

"Your parents were hoarders?" I was trying to wrap my head around the fact that my family tree was messy down to the roots.

"I grew up with it," she said. "I guess that's why I didn't see it in your father until it was so out of hand."

"Was Daddy always like this?"

"Oh, no. When we first moved in together, long before you were born, he was the complete opposite. We had this light green carpet that he obsessed over keeping clean. If anyone stepped on it with shoes on, he was there with a sponge, washing up their footsteps."

"When did he start collecting things?" I wondered how different my life would have been if my father was still obsessed with keeping things clean.

"When we left the Bronx," she told me. "It was like he had too much space."

"You know, I read that hoarding could be genetic," I said. A marker on chromosome 14 had been found in families where hoarding was common. "They say that all it takes is a trauma to set people off."

My mother knew where I was going with this. "Kim, I think you've been traumatized enough for one lifetime," she told me. "If you haven't started hoarding by now, you probably won't."

"Thanks."

"Oh, I didn't tell you about my new dentist," she said, deciding to change the topic. "He's very good-looking; he looks like the redhead from *The Partridge Family*."

"Danny Bonaduce?"

"I'm going to bring your picture with me to my next appointment."

"You want to set me up with a guy that looks like Danny Bonaduce?"

Since she had recovered from her surgery, my mother had become obsessed with my dating life, or lack thereof.

I had dated plenty of guys since breaking up with Paul, but had kept each relationship casual, ending things before *I love you*s could be whispered or family dinners expected. I figured there was a certain amount of emotional honesty and vulnerability that was required for relationships to be successful, and I was aware that there were things about myself, the things that made me most vulnerable, that shouldn't be shared over sushi or during pillow talk.

The only family I could imagine having was the one I already had, and while I loved them, I couldn't even fathom the kind of person who would willfully join it.

"I think you should call Dr. Philipps' office and make an appointment," my mom said

"For what?"

"A date. I think he liked you," she giggled. My mother had dedicated much of her surgical recovery stay in the hospital to setting me up with her surgeon, much to Dr. Philipps and my mutual embarrassment. "He offered to come to Brooklyn for a checkup. I'm sure he wouldn't do that for all of his patients."

"I try to make it a practice not to date men who have seen my mother naked."

"Think about how good you would look in comparison," she teased. "What about JDate? I'll pay for it. Jews make the best husbands."

"How would you know? You married two Catholics!"

"That's how I know. Don't make the same mistakes I have."

I promised my mother that I would sign up for a dating site. And when my parents dropped me off at home I followed through, signing up for the religiously unspecific — and more important, free — OKCupid.

After what seemed like hours of taking addictive tests about my vacation preferences, political leanings, and socializing inclinations, the first profile that came up in my matches was Dr. Philipps — we were, according to some sort of algorithm, a 98 percent match. From his profile, I learned that he was a recent transplant to New York, which I knew from researching him on the hospital website, that he liked cooking and reading, and had a dog.

If life were a movie, this would have been the moment when the music started and I hopped on a train, ran to his office, and professed my love for the doctor who saved my mother's life. But life was not a movie. I immediately disabled my account so that he couldn't see that I was looking at his page.

A few minutes passed, and then I joined JDate.

THIRTY-FOUR

WHEN BECKY AND ABBY ASKED me how my parents were doing, I lied, telling them they were doing great, that they had really made the effort to keep the place clean. But in reality, by the time summer had rolled around, Anna, Rachel, and I had already purged their apartment of hundreds of bags of paper.

The cleaning had become harder. The nightmares, the memories, the fact that so many people had volunteered their time and money to help them have a better life, only to have them squander it with the remnants of newsstands and clearance aisles, was all harder to bear. I didn't have the energy to make their home spotless again, so I settled on clean enough not to get evicted.

A stream of excuses and apologies erupted from my mother when she and my father returned from being out of the way: *I'm too weak to keep up with the cleaning. You know how Dad is. I'm so sorry you girls needed to do this again.* My father just stood behind her, smiling but miserable. After my friends left he immediately made the rounds, assessing the damage. Eventually he settled on the couch and started to rifle through the documents I had deemed important enough to keep.

I sat down next to him on the newly cleared couch, but he didn't look at me, too preoccupied with calculating what he was missing. "Would you rather I didn't clean your house out, Daddy?"

"No, it's good that you punish me."

I knew that was how he felt, like I was punishing him for being a bad boy. Punishing him for something he didn't quite understand was wrong.

"I'm not trying to punish you," I told him. "I'm just trying to prevent you from burying yourself alive."

"In an ideal world, there'd be a happy medium," he said, finally turning his attention toward me. "But, for now I'd rather you kept me from ending up like one of the Collyer brothers. Which one of them died buried in the house?"

"They both did."

My parents were in their mid-sixties, but time had been hard on them. As angry as I was, I still worried all the time about what would happen if one of them died. If my father died first, I was petrified that my mother would be too embarrassed by whatever mess he left behind to let anyone in the house to get him. If she were to go first, I was relatively sure he would end up exactly like the Collyer brothers, swallowed whole in a sea of paper.

"Dad, did you know how bad the old house was?"

"You know, I couldn't see it when we were in it," he said. "But when I look back on it . . . how do I put this . . . it was suffocating."

. . .

I had been able to staple my box spring back together successfully but I had put the rest of my furniture out on the curb during my bedbug paranoia. The upside to being underfurnished was that I could redecorate. The mismatched furniture that my parents picked up for me over the years had served me well, but it was time to move on to mostly matching and slightly more fancy knock-down furniture.

My parents offered their help building my new IKEA furniture and painting my walls. I wasn't entirely sold on putting them to work, but it would be nice to have company while I painted my cream-colored walls blue.

By the time my parents arrived, I had dutifully studied the art of painting on YouTube, watching every video about proper painting protocol I could find. I removed what remained of my furniture, cleaned, cleaned again, laid out old sheets, and taped all of the corners of the room in accordance with the instructions bestowed to me by various Internet gurus.

I had a plan for how I wanted the day's work to go. First, we would paint the perimeters of the walls, since that's what the Internet had told me to do, and then we would fill in the gaps. I tried to explain my strategy, but my parents were excited and rolled their rollers in all sorts of non–strategically approved places — happy to be helping. I bit my tongue and reminded myself that they had driven to Brooklyn to help me. When the sponge from my father's roller flew off the handle and rolled across my wood floors, I kicked them out of the bedroom, turned on a movie in my living room, made them a snack, and banished them from reentering the bedroom.

I wanted to paint my room, and I wanted it to be beautiful

and perfect and structured and not like everything else we did as a family.

After about an hour, my back was starting to hurt, and I could have used the extra help. I was far too stubborn to let them back in, though. Luckily, when my father's snoring had gotten so loud that it drowned out the television, my mother knocked on my door.

"Honey, can I come in? I'll listen to your directions."

"Sorry. I'm . . ."

"A control freak." She finished my sentence for me, but that wasn't what I was going to say. "I know. I made you, remember?"

She was silent for a moment. "Kim, what's going on with you? The bedbug calls in the middle of the night, the hives, the fact that you appear to no longer own furniture?"

"I've been having nightmares."

No matter how angry I would get at my mother, I still told her everything, but I hadn't yet told her about my cleaning night-mares. I didn't want her to feel any guiltier than she already did.

I told her about my dreams, about how no matter how much research I did or therapy I went to I couldn't make them stop. I told her about the sludge and the bugs I saw every time I closed my eyes. I told her I remembered all of these things that I hadn't thought about in years.

She listened to it all while slowly painting. "We shouldn't have had you. That was no way for a child to live," she said quietly.

I was surprised by that response — before her surgery, my mom would have given me a pep talk about putting my child-hood behind me. "I'm glad you did. I like me," I backpedalled.

"You wouldn't have known the difference," she said. "I remember the moment that I started hoarding, too. I wanted space for myself in my own house, so I started acting like him. I was a terrible mother."

"You were not a terrible mother. It was a terrible situation, but it's over now." If she didn't want to be her optimistic self, I would.

"It will never be over."

I had always wondered what had changed my mom. My mother wasn't like my father — she bought stuff, but she saw the squalor around them. But old habits die hard, even habits carefully chosen out of spite.

THIRTY-FIVE

I PROMISED MY MOTHER that I would use the three-strike rule in regard to Internet dating. I would date three guys, the first three on JDate I deemed worthy of real life communication, and after that I would be allowed to give up and wither and die alone.

The first, David number one, was promising. He accidentally told me that he loved me on our fourth date, and I let it slide, playing it off as if I hadn't heard the premature declaration. Sweet, Canadian, and a doctor — he was the kind of guy I wanted to want to end up with; he loved his family and wanted one of his own. He talked about "people like us" as if I fit into the same social hierarchy he came from. I could tell he had grown up with money by the way he spoke and dressed and the fact that he had finished medical school without student loans, but I didn't realize how much money until he took me to a hockey game and casually mentioned that his family were partial owners of the team we were watching.

I broke up with him that night. I didn't want to date this great guy for the wrong reasons. I told him he was practically perfect, but I wasn't feeling what I should. He told me I *was* perfect. And that was the problem — I wasn't, and I didn't want to pretend I was anymore.

David number two only got one date. Ivy League–educated and with excellent email banter skills, he texted me thirty minutes before our date: *BTW, I have a glass eye. I hope that won't be an issue.*

No worries, I replied. *I highlight my hair — it's not naturally striped.*

The glass eye didn't bother me; it was the fact that David number two had lied by omission. He was paralyzed on one half of his body, including his vocal cords. I smiled and tried to guess when to laugh throughout our date, but I couldn't understand anything he'd said.

My last date, the final date I had to go through with before I could officially tell my mother that I was through with online dating, was with Roy.

Roy. I said the name over and over again, trying to make sense of it. Simple, but not exactly popular in my generation. I expected men named Roy to more closely resemble my father's potbellied coworkers than this guy. In his online profile pictures, Roy had a square jaw, dimples, dark hair, and a seemingly ever-present tan. Roy looked more like he should be walking a runway than driving a bus. And Roy was kind of funny.

I had assumed that his profile was fake, a plant set up by the company to entice members to renew their plans when they were running out, but Roy didn't send me a form email. He responded to my profile as if he had actually read it.

I wanted to be honest on my JDate profile, so I wrote, "They say you'll know what a woman will look like in thirty years by looking at her mother. Unfortunately for you, I look like my father, which means in thirty years I'll bear a striking resemblance to Santa Claus."

Roy's pickup email said, "The original Santa Claus was Turkish, you know."

I wrote back that I was far too fair-skinned to pass as Mediterranean and would have to resolve to spend my latter years in a crushed red velvet pantsuit.

We continued our JDate banter for a few more days before he asked if he could see me in person. At this point, I'd already had my fill of the dating scene. But I had made a promise to my mother and was admittedly curious about this Roy character. As far as looks went, he was out of my league, and to verify that fact I forwarded his pictures to everyone I knew, including my parents, to ask if he was too attractive to date.

"Your dad says he looks Photoshopped," my mom emailed back.

Roy walked right past me, and when I called out for him he looked back at me with what I assumed to be disappointment. "Kim?"

He assured me that he overlooked me because I was blonder in real life than I looked in my photographs. I didn't believe him, but followed him to the Thai restaurant he'd picked out for our midday date anyway. I'd already written him off.

Over vegetarian duck, Roy filled me in on his life: grad student, native Israeli, personal trainer. "I have a green card," he volunteered, probably noting my uncontrollably furrowed brow. "I'm not using you for citizenship." Roy was a writer, too. When he was finished with grad school, he told me, he wanted to write children's books.

I gave my first-date spiel: I lived in Brooklyn, freelanced as an actress and also as a writer, and had two kooky parents whom I adored that lived two hours east of the city.

"What do you write?" he asked.

"Well, I write gossip and fitness stuff mostly, but I've been writing a bunch of personal essays. Not to publish, necessarily, more for myself."

"About . . ."

"About my past," I said, unsure of how to proceed. I wasn't sure why I was being so honest with this guy — maybe because I'd already made up my mind that there would be no second date.

"What about your past?"

"Well, I'm writing about my family — my dad has an obsessive compulsive disorder." That was only partially true, but I didn't feel like launching into the newest theories that hoarding is not really an OCD but its own compulsive behavioral disorder.

"Does he wash his hands a lot?"

"No." *Here goes nothing.* "He's a hoarder."

He looked at me for a minute, considering what he'd just heard, and promptly asked for the check.

I expected an awkward hug in the front of the restaurant and then a ritualistic turning to walk separate directions . . . regardless of where we were each headed next. But Roy just held his elbow out for me to hold and walked me to the Strand.

We spent about an hour picking through the aisles of the iconic bookstore. In the graphic novel section, I learned that Roy was a comic book geek. A really sexy comic book geek.

In trade, I admitted my soft spot for urban fantasy novels, confessing that more than a respectable share of my reading

consists of vampires, werewolves, and faeries of various disposi-
tions. I wasn't sure if I was more embarrassed by my father or
my reading habits, but I was being completely and utterly honest
about who I was with this Israeli Comic-Con aficionado.

After the bookstore we ate ice cream in the park, and then
when it started to rain, we sat in a café.

I told him I wasn't looking for anything serious. I'd had a boss
once who had a plaque over her desk that said MANAGE EXPEC-
TATIONS, and I wanted to make sure neither Roy nor I expected
anything to come of this five-hour date.

"I'd like to change your mind," he said, not being managed in
the slightest.

I gave him a kiss on the cheek and left one café to immediately take up residence in another and call my mother.

"Don't gloat, but I had a good date."

"David?"

"No, Roy."

"Roy," she said. "That's funny, on your first birthday cake, the
bakery misspelled your name — they wrote an *o* instead of an *l*.
We called you Kimberoy for the entire year."

It took exactly four dates for the topic of hoarding to come up
again. All of our dates had been epically long, and this one was
no different. A lunch date had turned into a 3 a.m. diner run, and
Roy wanted to know more about my childhood.

"What does your father hoard?"

"Paper, but more than paper. I don't know how to describe
it," I said. "He loves information so much, but it gets so out of
hand."

"Just paper doesn't seem that bad."

"No, it doesn't. Like I said, I don't know how to describe it.

I'll send you some of the essays I've been writing. Somehow it's easier for me to put it all down on paper than to say it all so that it makes sense."

A few days later I got a text from Roy, who I was officially more than comfortably giddy about.

Roy's Droid: Just finished reading.

Kim's iPhone: Still like me?

Roy's Droid: Yes. Respect you even more.

Kim's iPhone: Thank you.

Roy's Droid: Heavy stuff. Some cringeworthy.

Kim's iPhone: Hence me being nervous about you reading it.

Roy's Droid: Well I'm damaged goods too so you ain't so special.

Roy's Droid: You're obviously very strong. I admire that.

Kim's iPhone: Thanks for your observations.

Roy's Droid: My observation is that you're all kinds of awesome
    & I'm excited to be with you.

On our next date Roy bought me a toothbrush and asked me if I would be his girlfriend, officially.

THIRTY-SIX

A FEW MONTHS AFTER our first date, Roy and I celebrated our first Halloween as a couple by throwing a party. I was busy putting coats in the bedroom while Roy chatted with our friends in the living room. I had a hanger between my teeth when Meghan, a relatively new friend I'd met while traveling earlier that year, came looking for me. "So, Roy mentioned you're writing about hoarding."

Pain shot through my jaw as I clenched down on the hanger. I realized that by telling Roy my father is a hoarder, he assumed I was the kind of person who regularly told people that my father is a hoarder.

"My mother's a hoarder," Meghan said, hurriedly.

I unclenched and nodded. "My father's a hoarder."

We hung out in my room, comparing stories like two grizzled war veterans.

"I just don't know why my father stays with her," she told me.

"I've thought that, too, about my mom. Although my mom isn't like your dad; she's sort of taken up hoarding as well." But I did know why her father stayed, and my mother stayed, and why we, as their children, stay. Life without their stuff just wasn't worth life without them.

My parents started looking for a new apartment almost as soon as my mother was released from the hospital. They quickly put a deposit down on a cute two-bedroom condo in a retirement community not far from where I grew up. The idea of my parents owning a home scared me; if they rented and their apartment belonged to and was maintained by other people, it meant a safeguard against squalor.

"If I own something, like this condo, I can leave it to you. And that means I won't have completely failed as a mother," my mom said when I talked to her about my fears about home ownership. Since her stay in the hospital, my mother had become obsessed with what would happen to me when she died. With my dating life under control, she'd set her sights on establishing some sort of inheritance for me.

I told her she was being ridiculous, as if I'd just been hanging around for the last twenty-eight years waiting for a windfall. All I wanted, all I had ever wanted, was for my family to live in a safe place, a place without shame. I hoped that this condo could be that for them.

The community seemed a bit Stepford-esque to me, the kind of place where you have to keep your car in the garage as opposed to filling it with garbage. Everyone's garden was perfectly kept and there were language clubs and dance classes and people went to themed formals at the clubhouse. It felt like boarding school for the over-sixty crowd. And their mortgage was far less per month than the rent they were paying at their old apartment complex. But the perks I was particularly happy about were the front-door garbage pickup, since it meant they actually had to put out garbage, and the bus service around town, which meant my mother no longer had to be a prisoner to my father's work schedule. She could grab the jitney to town to shop or people-watch of her own volition.

But after putting the deposit down on the new condo, my parents' mortgage application was among the many things lost in the to-do piles of failing mortgage companies. Their closing date was put off again and again and again, while one bank was busy buying another. It gave them increasingly more time to stockpile in the apartment they were waiting to move out of; it became just as bad if not worse than it was a year and a half earlier, when I begged my friends to help me make it safe for my mother.

Technically, they could have closed on the condo a few months before, but there was the issue of packing. They extended their lease of the apartment by a month, twice. My mom told me, "I just need more time to pack." Which meant of course that she needed someone else to pack for her.

We had been doing this dance for years. I rolled my eyes when my mother talked about needing more time to pack. Luckily, she couldn't see me, because all of our conversations now took place over the phone. I cut back on my visits home; the most convenient excuse I had was that I was busy trying to figure out how to survive financially. The Web show had a good run but was cancelled when the magazine industry was hit hard by the recession. I had been picking up lots of little jobs to stay afloat, with the workload and overdue invoices to prove it. There were also other, less understandable excuses: that I was in love and wanted to spend my weekends cuddling at home or cavorting about town with my man.

But the truth was that I just couldn't stand being around my parents anymore. That year marked the angriest in my existence. The mass cleanout that we did before my mom came home from the hospital changed something in me. I'd cleaned out my parents' apartment so many times, but that time was different. I had been keeping my parents' secret for so long that the shame associated with it defined me, and when they needed me to, I aired out everything I had been ashamed of my entire life for the world to see — and then my parents had screwed it all up again. I had had to do complete overhauls of my parents' apartment twice since then, and I knew my parents needed me to do it again. But I didn't have it in me.

When our conversation inevitably turned to the topic of how overwhelmed my mom was and how much work she'd done and how my father was no help at all, I gave her the names and numbers of companies and individuals that advertised cleaning and packing services in her area. I even offered to pay. I would pay anything not to have to go home.

She told me she'd call them when she was ready. But she was never going to be ready, so I nagged.

"Are you showing off to your friends?" she said when I called to ask if she'd called the cleaning woman I'd recommended.

"No." The fact that my parents needed professional help to pack their apartment, the fact that they had mounds of trash and clutter everywhere, the fact that they lived like hobos in their own home, weren't exactly the things I bragged about. But my mom certainly knew what buttons to push. Her question made me furious. And then it made me feel guilty for being angry with her. I didn't feel I had the right to, any more than the child of a paraplegic getting angry with their parent for not walking. I calmed myself down.

"I'm calling to see if you've done it. Do you want me to call? Will it be less embarrassing if I explain the situation?"

"Maybe. I don't know. Do you want to?"

"What's your budget?" I asked.

"I'll call when I'm ready. Good-bye, honey." She hung up on me.

My aunt attempted to take up the slack that was usually my responsibility, coming out on the weekends to do my domestic duties. Lee had already complained to me between visits that nothing was being added to the pile of packed boxes. One night she texted me: *There's a lot left for you to do, good luck.*

My mom called a few days later, just as I was packing my suitcase to head out to the Island. It was a big weekend: Rachel and Tim were getting married and my parents were meeting Roy for the first time — without me. I'd be busy taking pictures with the bridal party during the cocktail hour and wouldn't be there to ref the first round of *Roy v. Parents.* Roy had already offered to discuss with my parents how important it was that I focused on work — I had a gargantuan project to finish — and not spend my weekends doing hoard management. I told him not to get involved. I'd rather he met my parents for the first time without putting them on the defensive.

"Hey, Mama, what's up?"

I heard my mother start laughing, even before she spoke.

"Your dad says you'll probably hit me, but I have an idea."

"What's the idea?"

"After the ceremony, maybe you and Roy could come over and help us move."

I was genuinely stunned. "Mom . . ."

"I thought it would be a good idea."

"Let me get this straight," I said, trying to cool myself down. "You want me to leave my best friends' wedding reception, skip their afterparty, and put my boyfriend, whom you have never met, to work cleaning and packing your house."

"Your dad said you'd react like this." She'd stopped laughing. "I'm sorry I'm not being supportive of you, but I need your help."

I didn't see how letting me enjoy my best friends' wedding in peace was being so magnanimously supportive. But I wasn't angry, just sorry. Sorry I wasn't being supportive of her. More than that, I was exhausted by the expectation that my family's functioning was my responsibility alone.

"Fine. I'll ride back into the city with Roy after the wedding, drop off my dress, and come back out the following day. I'll give you a week, but if you don't do anything, I don't do anything." I told her. "I'm not doing this alone. Rachel and Tim will be on their honeymoon, and frankly I'm sick of asking her and Anna to clean your apartment. You have no idea how humiliating that is for me."

"You don't think I'm humiliated?"

Apparently not humiliated enough to hire someone to help as opposed to taking advantage of my friends. But I knew that to her, my friends were like family — they already knew what they were getting into. Hiring someone was just inviting judgment.

It had always been easier for me to be mad at my mother than my father. She was a fighter and she could take it, and she'd love me anyway. I wasn't sure my dad could take the brunt of my anger. And beyond that, he had never asked for my help. He didn't know the right buttons to push to make me feel like a terrible daughter. He didn't start crying on the phone about how helpless he was, so that I'd do what needed to be done.

Although my father had no plans to change his behavior, he would not throw a hissy fit if his belongings were thrown out. He had even requested — on his own, amazingly enough — that they hire a cleaning person to come in regularly.

My mother, on the other hand, was forever ruled by embarrassment. Any progress we made when she helped me paint my apartment had long been forgotten. She once again insisted that the entire mass of mess was still all my father's fault, and that she never bought anything.

I took the week after Rachel's wedding off from work, assuming that I wouldn't have time to wake up in the morning and write about celebrity gossip or the best beer gardens in New York while moving my parents. But my first three days home were a waste. I tried sticking to my guns and not doing anything because no one else was, but by the time Wednesday arrived, I realized that it just wasn't going to happen. The apartment was worse than I had ever seen it; there were piles reaching all the way to the ceiling now, like columns, and not only did I have to sort through those piles, I had to pack their contents and move them. So I swallowed my pride and called Abby again.

"Hey, lady, it's Kim."

"Hey, hon. How's the move going?" Abby asked.

"That's why I'm calling. Do you think I could hire Reina to help me again?"

"Let me call my mom. I'll get back to you."

"Thanks. And sorry."

"No worries. I'm sure she could use the extra money for Christmas shopping."

I hung up and called Anna. At the wedding, she had offered to help. I told her "absolutely not," but I needed all the help I could get.

"I can do Saturday, but I have plans on Sunday," she told me.

"I'm trying to hire someone to help for Sunday, so that should work. Thanks for doing this again. I'm sorry."

"I had a feeling you might call. I'll see you Saturday."

It was four days before they needed to be out, and my mom was just getting around to hiring movers. I had asked that she make those calls while I was arranging for help. When I was done begging my friends, I went into her room to check on the status of that chore, only to have her tell me that it was far too expensive. "Maybe we'll just rent one of those trucks from Home Depot and do it ourselves."

Clean. Pack. And now move. I had my work cut out for me. I started with the guest room, which I'd designated as my room. For some reason, because it was my room, my parents insisted that the mess that resided there was my mess. But the only thing I kept in there was a Yaffa block full of underwear and pajamas. The room was a catchall for junk, reminding me of my grandparents' unused room. There were infomercial exercise devices; boxes of towels and sheets that were never unpacked from their last move; the mini-fridge I bought when I went to college, now full of the food that my parents couldn't fit in the kitchen fridge; a cabinet reserved solely for porcelain dolls my mother bought from television shopping channels but would never display and never sell even though she insisted they were an investment; a rotisserie; scrapbooking kits; pots, pans, cookie cutters, and extra blenders; and the boxes and bags of papers that my father had strategically placed throughout it all. I knew that if I started here I'd have very little interruption. No one would peek out and tell me that whatever it was I was holding was incredibly important for some far-reaching reason, that they had been looking for those towels for the past five years or that there's a check lost in one of those bags of papers they'd like me to find.

Abby called back. Reina was sick, but Abby's mother and two aunts were going to come help on Sunday.

"Thank you. I'm so sorry to be doing this again." I told her. "How much should we set aside?"

"Nothing. Don't worry about it."

I shook my head, as if she could hear me do it. "Abby, I'm not letting them come here and clean this mess for nothing!"

"Don't worry, they just got a big bonus from one of the rich-people clients. They're just sharing the wealth."

I paid my cleaning lady $100 for my apartment, so I resolved to tell my mother that that was what we were paying each woman who helped us — perhaps not as a fee, but Abby didn't say anything about tipping.

We threw out at least seventy bags of trash — an entire roll of heavy-duty garbage bags — on Saturday alone. But there was still so much work to be done that Anna cancelled her Sunday plans and returned Sunday morning. Reina apparently felt better and showed up with the rest of Abby's mother's crew.

"We've been cleaning for days," I told Abby's mom in the parking lot when she pulled in. "It just doesn't look like it."

"Don't worry."

"Anna and I are going to spend today loading the truck and bringing things to the new place. Maybe you can stay here with my parents and help with what's left."

I felt yet again like I was taking the easy way out. I hated leaving other people to do the cleaning. But before Abby came, I reached a breaking point. Upon moving the still-unpacked boxes from their last move, I found that hundreds of pill bugs had made their home in the guest room, *my room*. Living and dead, the bugs were clustered together under a plastic shelving unit that held towels no one had used in years. I was drained, physically and emotionally, and I couldn't take this new find. I marched over to my parents, who were huddled over the bags of stuff I'd already bundled up for a trip to their complex dumpster.

"If you ever put me in this situation again, I am done with you."

I'd been mad before, but never this livid. I refused to have to ask my friends for help again. I wanted them to take responsibility for themselves, for their own home, but it was too much to ask. Their brains didn't work that way. Embarrassment wasn't enough of a motivator. Nothing was enough of a motivator, except maybe losing me. It took a bottle of painkillers to get them out of their last dump. This time, I would be leaving them by my own choice. No more monthly requests that I come home to help.

My dad's head sunk into his shoulders, and he started to twiddle his thumbs nervously, but he didn't say anything. My words rolled off of my mom like Teflon. "I know you're mad now, but in two weeks you'll love me again," she said.

I loved her then; that wasn't the point. I wouldn't put myself through all of that if I didn't love her. But I was done cleaning up after her and my father, done with being done and then returning. So now, I informed her, I was passing the buck to my friend's mother, who was nice or crazy enough to come to my rescue.

Anna, my dad, and I loaded up the truck from noon to midnight, taking trip after trip to the new apartment. I mopped and scrubbed the new place so that it'd be a clean start for my parents, and I tried to unpack as many boxes as I could before they arrived so that those things wouldn't stay in boxes and become hideouts for bugs.

Abby's mother's van pulled up to the house with the last of the stuff shortly after midnight.

"Thank you. You really didn't have to stay this late."

"We didn't want to leave you. You have your hands full."

"I really can't thank you enough."

I meant it, but I was also simply going through the motions. I had said it all before. It was a never-ending cycle: each time feeling helpless, then angry, then guilty, then frustrated, then resigned, ad infinitum, ad absurdum.

Abby's family and Anna left, and then it was just me and my parents.

"Your father and I have talked about it, and we really want to surprise you. We're going to keep this place nice. When you come to visit next time, you'll be proud."

"I believe in you," I said, telling them what I had always told them, but this time it was lip service. I didn't believe in them. They would mess up the next place, then the next, and the one after that. One day they would die and I would do one final cleaning and it would finally be over. If I made peace with anything, it was that my parents were never going to change.

"If you believed in us, it wouldn't be a surprise. It's okay. We wouldn't believe in us either."

THIRTY-SEVEN

WHEN I GOT BACK to Brooklyn from a solid week of cleaning, packing, and moving, I was depleted. I wanted nothing more than to curl up in the fetal position and cry for three to four months. But I had to get back to work. I had deadlines to meet and pitches to send out.

Roy came over; for once, I was unwilling to head to Manhattan to see him. I needed to be in my own meticulously maintained space. Over the course of our six-month relationship, his place had become our place, and my place remained mine. That was how I preferred it.

Craving vegetables, anything that was not typical moving food — pizza, soda, Taco Bell — I headed to the kitchen to make dinner.

When I turned around, butcher knife in hand, Roy was on one knee.

No.

"Kimberly Rae Miller," he began, "from our first date, I knew I never wanted to be with anyone else. I plan on spending my life with you . . ."

I'm holding a knife. I'm holding a knife. I'm holding a knife.

" . . . so I was thinking we could start by moving in together."

Eventually I started breathing again, although it took longer than expected. I was so glad he didn't ask me to marry him. I think I would have said yes, but I would have been really pissed off about it — I wanted to be with this guy forever, but I was not romantic enough to feel comfortable with committing to someone after only six months of dating.

I didn't tell him this. I didn't tell him anything. I just stared at him like he was a lunatic. He stared back, grinning from ear to ear. He knew me, knew how I'd react, and he was very pleased with himself for nearly giving me a stroke.

"What if we have too much stuff?" was my response.

"You can throw out all of my stuff . . . except for my comic books." The smart, beautiful, accepting man who I was in love with just happened to collect paper. There was an irony there that didn't escape me. It also petrified me.

"What are you going to do with the comic books?"

"We'll find storage. I promise you that they will never take over. You never have to worry about that, Kim."

"Okay."

"Okay?"

"Okay. I'll move in with you — but not yet. In six months. I think a year is a good amount of time to be together before moving in."

"Ha, okay. In six months," he said, content. "You should have seen the look on your face when you thought I was going to propose."

"You're lucky I didn't stab you."

Before I knew it, six months had passed, and soon enough Roy and I were looking at real estate. We each had our nonnegotiable must-haves: I wanted a real kitchen, since cooking is the thing that relaxes me the most, and I didn't want a stove in the middle of my living room. He was adamant about living in Manhattan. His argument: "I did not travel 6,000 miles from the other side of planet Earth to *not* live in New York City."

I tried explaining that Manhattan was one of the five boroughs that make up New York City. Brooklyn was another one. But Roy would have none of it.

We compromised — I agreed to move to Manhattan for the next few years, but once kids were in the picture, we were hightailing it back to Brooklyn. Roy agreed to agree, for now.

Our first day of hunting made it very, very clear that New York City was chock-full of overpriced slumlike apartments. Well-maintained high-rises were out of our price range, even with each of us willing to pay what we already did in rent. I paid the same amount for my two-bedroom apartment in Park Slope that Roy did for his posh Upper West Side shoebox studio. I had assumed that the combined force of both our rents would allow us to upgrade, but the apartments in our price range were musty, ill-kempt walkups with narrow hallways and smoke-stained walls.

I was starting to feel anxious about the whole moving in together thing. We could have a successful bi-borough relationship forever, maybe. When we had kids we could trade off days. It worked for divorced people. It's amazing the things you convince yourself of when you're apartment hunting in New York.

Two weeks and nearly thirty apartments later, I got a text message from Lee. A coworker of hers lived in Chelsea, one of the city's trendiest neighborhoods, and there was an apartment for rent in his building that was, surprisingly, in our range.

The real estate agent ushered us in, apologizing for the state of the apartment, which was in the middle of renovation. "The guy who lived here was a hoarder," he said matter-of-factly, assuring us that the dead roach carcasses on the walls would be scraped off, a new bathroom sink would be installed, and a fresh coat of paint would wash away all signs of the previous tenant.

I knew what Roy was thinking. The place was perfect. It would be newly renovated, it was relatively spacious, and it was exactly the right location and exactly the right price. I wanted to see what he saw in the apartment, but all I saw were the roaches on the walls.

I shelved those thoughts. I told him that we should take it, to go ahead and put down a deposit, because it's perfect for us. And by *us*, I meant *him*. Nothing in our price range would be perfect for me. I really wanted to make him happy.

I couldn't sleep that night. I lay awake in Roy's bed, crying. I knew he didn't fully understand what home meant to me, the kind of weight it carried. He'd moved practically every year since he came to New York seven years ago. An apartment was a place to put his stuff, but to me home was something to be defined by. I grew up ashamed of who I was, because my home was something to be ashamed of. I had never been more proud of anything in my life than I'd been of the tiny Brooklyn apartment I was leaving to start a life with Roy — it was small and clean and *mine*, and for so much of my life that was all I ever wanted. I didn't know what kind of apartment would define us, but I was pretty sure the apartment in Chelsea, with its dead roach carcasses, wasn't it.

Around 3 a.m. I snuck out and took a cab home to Brooklyn. I needed to be with myself, with my stuff. Understandably, he was angry when he woke up and I wasn't there.

"You can't just sneak off in the middle of the night. What are you going to do when we live together?"

"Sneak off to the living room," I said, crying.

"It was the hoarding thing, wasn't it?" he said. "I could see it in your face when he said it. I should have known."

"I'm sorry."

"Don't be. Losing a deposit isn't the worst thing. But I do expect you to pay for it."

"Okay." My crying had slowed down to snivels.

"I'll email the real estate agent about the uptown apartment; I'll tell her we'll take it."

It was an apartment I actually really liked and Roy really didn't. It was large and beautiful and had a full modern kitchen, but it was also expensive and much farther uptown than we'd planned. The agent told us she could get the paperwork started early the next day, but first she had one last apartment to show us — it had just become available and was only slightly over budget and just a few blocks from Roy's current apartment.

We went to look at it on the way to signing for the other one, just in case. Even as we walked down the block, Roy shot me an impressed look. The street was picturesque, classic New York: turn-of-the-last-century four-story brownstones, with arched entryways and bow windows and Romanesque flourishes. The street was quiet and canopied by two rows of trees, ending at a small park.

We were greeted by the landlord, who lived on the first floor. Various members of his extended family occupied most of the other apartments in the building. It being the Upper West Side, he was, unsurprisingly, a nice old Jewish man, and he seemed to be taken by us, especially Roy, the young man from the homeland. He seemed to be less interested in showing us around than testing his Hebrew out on Roy.

As a large prewar brownstone, the apartment was not the brand-spanking-new luxury building one I thought I wanted, but it was a very far cry from the roach carcass–covered apartment in Chelsea. It was elegant. It had 12-foot ceilings, a built-in fireplace with a carved mantel, and giant bow windows with old-fashioned wood shutters. The cabinets and appliances were a wee bit dated, but I let Roy do the negotiating. They chatted in Hebrew for a while, eventually agreeing on a new refrigerator, bathroom sink, and significant reduction in rent.

"The bedroom is big enough for a queen-size bed," I yelled out. Roy came in to check.

"We could have a crib here too," he said.

"We could," I replied, about our hypothetical offspring. "But when the kid needs a bed we're going back to Brooklyn."

"Deal."

I woke up from a nightmare shortly after 3 a.m. I thought about waking Roy, but he'd already been subjected to too many nightmare-induced sleepless nights.

We had spent the day buying up the entire contents of IKEA (or as Roy insisted, "European imports") for our new apartment. It was an exhausting day of shopping and carrying heavy things, so I let him sleep and stared at the ceiling until it was time for me to tiptoe out to meet my aunt. We'd scheduled an early-morning wine tasting on Long Island.

When Roy heard the bedroom door squeak open, he called out for me. I knew he was thinking that I was running away in the middle of the night again.

"I'm not leaving you; I'm leaving to meet Lee."

"You were tossing and turning again last night."

"Nightmare," I said.

"What was this one about?"

"Same thing, different night. We were in the house I grew up in, but my parents weren't there," I told him. "It was our house now, but it was just as bad. I was looking out the window of my childhood bedroom into the neighbor's yard, admiring how nicely it was kept. In the dream they had two swimming pools: fresh water and chlorinated. Apparently we were engaged, and a newspaper was coming to do a wedding announcement, and we had to clean. I didn't know where to start. You told me you had hired people, and I said 'I don't have to do it myself?' You said no, I didn't have to do it at all, and then I said, 'This is who I am, this is what made me.' Then I woke up."

He sat up, still groggy. "That's not who you are. I will never let that happen. You will always live somewhere you're proud of."

Upper West Side

Epilogue

W HEN I DECIDED to write my story, I thought I would make it a research-heavy book and throw in intermittent personal anecdotes as support. All of this was a plan to both understand and accept my parents. Secretly, though, I hoped that I might figure out a way to fix them. I fantasized that I would soon be calling home with a little nugget of information that would click for them, and all of a sudden they would hate owning things.

That didn't happen, of course. I didn't write a research-heavy book, and I didn't figure out how to fix them. They still loved stuff. But I kept writing my story, and in doing so, something else happened: I figured out that I can be mad at my parents. Really mad. And I learned that in spite of my anger, they would still love me, and I would still love them. They can't clean the moldy spots on my childhood, but they can serve as my cheering section, and they always have. Both of my parents have supported this process in ways that I had never expected.

I've talked to my mother almost every day since the inception of this book — to check dates and facts and details, but also to cry.

"Kim, you're out. It's over. We all survived that place," my mother said when I called crying about some long-lost memory I hid away.

My father learned the art of text messaging, sending me virtual shoulder-rubs and "You can do this, kiddo" messages during breaks in his shift.

He started taking writing classes, because, he now says, he's always liked writing. "You take after me like that."

I told him that his first book should be a rebuttal. He can talk about the time I peed in the car or the time I washed his car with Brillo pads, or the time I climbed a tree but made him get a ladder to come get me, because I realized I was scared of heights once I was up there.

When my book proposal was finished and ready to be sent off to my agent, he asked if he could read it. I sat with him as he did, watching his face for any signs that he'd hate me. But when he looked up, he said, "Wow, that's quite a story. I'm sorry that it was yours."

I have never needed an apology from my parents. I have only ever wanted them to have a safe place to live. As I write this, my parents have been in their new home for over a year. It is clean, so far. It has not been easy, though. My mother has attempted to curtail her compulsive shopping by writing a shopping blog, which has a decent following, where she scopes out Internet sales on a daily basis and passes them on to others for the same rush of the buy. Sometimes that works. Sometimes she calls me and says, "I've had a rough week and I bought too much."

My father has promised to go to therapy. I'm not sure if he ever really will, but he has been calling therapists, looking for someone who not only has experience with hoarding but also takes insurance — a combination that is genuinely hard to find. My mom says he actually sounds excited whenever I check in on his therapist search.

As a housewarming present, I bought them a day with a professional organizer. The woman I hired was an amazon compared to my tiny mother, and for weeks afterward I received phone calls along the lines of "I can't reach my plates! Who puts the plates on the top shelf?!"

A cleaning person comes regularly, if nothing else but to scare my parents into putting things away before she arrives.

Nothing about this is easy for my parents. My mom likes to call me a few times a week to tell me about the strange places my dad has been hiding bundles of papers that he thinks she won't find. On recycling day she wakes up at 5 a.m. to scour their house and garage for bags of papers to put out before my father can get up and reclaim them.

"I don't know how long I can do this," she told me. "You'll have to start having kids soon so that they will love me before I get too tired of cleaning up after your father and let it fall apart again."

Roy and I have settled into our new place. The walls are decorator white and summer-shower blue and the furniture is mostly coffee brown, the colors we both agreed on. I keep my girlier, more flowery stuff contained in my office nook in our bedroom; he keeps his comic book paraphernalia on his office wall and in the library in the living room. His boxes upon boxes of comic books (thirty, at present count) have found a home in a storage unit. Our apartment is tasteful and clean and presentable. It's very much home.

My favorite part about it is that right outside our window is a stop for the M5, the bus my father used to drive when I was a little girl. I like to sit by the stop to call my parents a few times each week. My dad never fails to have a story about pickpockets, the bakery owner who used to trade him artisanal loaves of bread in exchange for a free ride, or the time he almost hit Aunt Lee when she walked in front of his bus. When it's my mother's turn, she tells me about her newest recipe, asks when I will come home to visit next, and worries that I'm not eating enough, wearing a sweater, saving enough money . . . the list goes on. These are the moments when I realize how very normal we are.

Acknowledgments

When I first met with Julia Cheiffetz and Carly Hoffmann at Amazon Publishing, Julia told me that writing this book would be the hardest thing I've ever done. She was right, and I can't imagine having done it without the constant guidance and encouragement you both provided in the process.

To my agent, Mollie Glick, thank you for believing in me and believing that I had a story to tell even before I told you what my story was.

Adrianna and Michelle, you are the two greatest blessings in my life. I can't imagine having grown up without you and am forever grateful for your support and friendship. Eddie, you're the best big brother this only child could ask for.

Thank you to all the friends, family, teachers, and various cohorts who have supported me in this process: MJ, Mark Goldstein, Yoselin Bugallo, Becky Gutierrez, Aziz Nekoukar, Amanda Figueroa, Michelle Slonim, Katharine Sise, Corey Binns, David Krell, Melanie Schutt, Johanna Saum, Vanessa Marmot, April Salazar Froncek, Kelly McMasters, Jill Schwartzman, Sarah McColl, Sebastian Conley, and all the readers of TheKimChallenge.com.

Roy Schwartz, thank you for being my happily ever after.

Most important, to my parents: You are the toughest, funniest, most wonderful people I know. I'm not sure that I can ever do you justice in words or thank you adequately for loving me enough to support me in writing this book. I am proud and thankful to be your daughter.

CPSIA information can be obtained
at www.ICGtesting.com
Printed in the USA
LVOW12s2300070118
562165LV00007B/597/P